AMERICA SEI

MW01533298

The Constitution
of the United States of America
Includes the Bill of Rights and Amendments 11-27

WORD SEARCH & CROSSWORD PUZZLE ACTIVITY

By Aisles of Books & Founding Fathers
(refer to page 7)

A fun and relaxing way for anyone looking to expand knowledge of our nation's Founding Documents

STUDENTS 🔔 HISTORY BUFFS 🔔 TEACHERS
🔔 PEOPLE OF ALL AGES 🔔

Includes
Fun and engaging Narratives, Word Activities & Trivia

DISCLAIMER

The puzzles, games and activities in this book are for entertainment purposes only. Although the author and publisher have worked to ensure that the information is accurate, the reader is being made aware that errors and/or omissions may occur. The author and publisher disclaim any liability to the person or party for any loss resulting from reliance on any information in this book.

Any references to historical events, real people, or real places are used fictitiously. Names, characters, and places are products of the author's imagination.

COPYRIGHT

America Series, The Constitution of the United States of America Word Search & Crossword Puzzle Activity Book: Includes the Bill of Rights and Amendments 11-27
1st Edition
The author is represented by: Aisles of Books
Contact: info@AislesOfBooks.club
Year of Publication: 2024
ISBN: 9798338334669
Head of Printing: Amazon KDP Publishing

CONTENTS

The Constitution, Bill of Rights and Amendments 11-27 (Founding Documents) are a public domain text from the holdings of the National Archives and Records Administration, Washington, DC. The authors of the Founding Documents are collectively and commonly known as "The Founding Fathers". Their names can be found at the end of each document or as specified therein.

The text of the Founding Documents is written using a formal "Type Writing" style.

Text that is not a part of the Founding Documents is written using a casual "Hand Writing" style.

The activities included in the pages of this book are designed to be fun and relaxing while helping you to explore the context of The Constitution of the United Sates of America.

We hope you find these activities enjoyable.

INSTRUCTIONS

The pages that follow contain word search and crossword puzzles. The words used to solve the puzzles are made available as following.

HIGHLIGHTED WORDS:
An exert from the text of The Constitution, Bill of Rights and Amendments may contain boldly **highlighted words**. The highlighted words can be used to directly solve the puzzle. Or, the word is an answer to a activity question that is also used to solve the puzzle.

QUESTIONS and FILL-IN THE BLANKS:
Some activities will ask questions about the Articles and Adendums. Answer them (or fill-in the blank ___?___) to help solve the puzzles.

SCRAMBLED WORDS:
Some activities have a list of scrambled words taken directly (and grammatically) from the Articles and Addendums. Unscramble them to help solve the puzzles.

PUZZLE DIFFICULTY LEVEL:
The difficulty level of each puzzle is indicated at the bottom of the page as follows.

EASY   MEDIUM   HARD

THE CONSTITUTION

RATIFIED

June 21, 1788

PURPOSE

To Constitution of the United States of America replaced the Articles of Confederation with a fresh governmental framework that enhanced and consolidated its authority. This new structure establishes policies and procedures to maintain a balance of power among its branches (executive, legislative, and judicial) and safeguards individual liberties. Additionally, it includes mechanisms for amending the document to accommodate evolving circumstances.

SIGNATORIES

39 of the 55 delegates.

We the People

of the United States, in order to form a more perfect Union, establish Justice, insure domestic Tranquility, provide for the common defence, promote the general Welfare, and secure the Blessings of Liberty to ourselves and our Posterity, do ordain and establish this Constitution for the United States of America.

Article. I.

Section. 1. All legislative Powers herein granted shall be vested in a Congress of the United States, which shall consist of a Senate and House of Representatives.

Section. 2. The House of Representatives shall be composed of Members chosen every second Year by the People of the several States, and the Electors in each State shall have the Qualifications requisite for Electors of the most numerous Branch of the State Legislature.

No Person shall be a Representative who shall not have attained to the Age of twenty five Years, and been seven Years a Citizen of the United States, and who shall not, when elected, be an Inhabitant of that State in which he shall be chosen.

Representatives and direct Taxes shall be apportioned among the several States which may be included within this Union, according to their respective Numbers, which shall be determined by adding to the whole Number of free Persons, including those bound to Service for a Term of Years, and excluding Indians not taxed, three fifths of all other Persons. The actual Enumeration shall be made within three Years after the first Meeting of the Congress of the United States, and within every subsequent Term of ten Years, in such Manner as they shall by Law direct. The Number of Representatives shall not exceed one for every thirty Thousand, but each State shall have at Least one Representative; and until such enumeration shall be made, the State of New Hampshire shall be entitled to chuse three, Massachusetts eight, Rhode-Island and Providence Plantations one, Connecticut five, New-York six, New Jersey four, Pennsylvania eight, Delaware one, Maryland six, Virginia ten, North Carolina five, South Carolina five, and Georgia three.

When vacancies happen in the Representation from any State, the Executive Authority thereof shall issue Writs of Election to fill such Vacancies.

The House of Representatives shall chuse their Speaker and other Officers; and shall have the sole Power of Impeachment.

Section. 3. The Senate of the United States shall be composed of two Senators from each State, chosen by the Legislature thereof, for six Years; and each Senator shall have one Vote.

Immediately after they shall be assembled in Consequence of the first Election, they shall be divided as equally as may be into three Classes. The Seats of the Senators of the first Class shall be vacated at the Expiration of the second Year, of the second Class at the Expiration of the fourth Year, and of the third Class at the Expiration of the sixth Year, so that one third may be chosen every second Year; and if Vacancies happen by Resignation, or otherwise, during the Recess of the Legislature of any State, the Executive thereof may make temporary Appointments until the next Meeting of the Legislature, which shall then fill such Vacancies.

No Person shall be a Senator who shall not have attained to the Age of thirty Years, and been nine Years a Citizen of the United States, and who shall not, when elected, be an Inhabitant of that State for which he shall be chosen.

The Vice President of the United States shall be President of the Senate, but shall have no Vote, unless they be equally divided.

The Senate shall chuse their other Officers, and also a President pro tempore, in the Absence of the Vice President, or when he shall exercise the Office of President of the United States.

The Senate shall have the sole Power to try all Impeachments. When sitting for that Purpose, they shall be on Oath or Affirmation. When the President of the United States is tried, the Chief Justice shall preside: And no Person shall be convicted without the Concurrence of two thirds of the Members present.

Judgment in Cases of Impeachment shall not extend further than to removal from Office, and disqualification to hold and enjoy any Office of Honor, Trust or Profit under the United States: but the Party convicted shall nevertheless be liable and subject to Indictment, Trial, Judgment and Punishment, according to Law.

Section. 4. The Times, Places and Manner of holding Elections for Senators and Representatives, shall be prescribed in each State by the Legislature thereof; but the Congress may at any time by Law make or alter such Regulations, except as to the Places of chusing Senators.

The Congress shall assemble at least once in every Year, and such Meeting shall be on the first Monday in December, unless they shall by Law appoint a different Day.

Section. 5. Each House shall be the Judge of the Elections, Returns and Qualifications of its own Members, and a Majority of each shall constitute a Quorum to do Business; but a smaller Number may adjourn from day to day, and may be authorized to compel the Attendance of absent Members, in such Manner, and under such Penalties as each House may provide.

Each House may determine the Rules of its Proceedings, punish its Members for disorderly Behaviour, and, with the Concurrence of two thirds, expel a Member.

Each House shall keep a Journal of its Proceedings, and from time to time publish the same, excepting such Parts as may in their Judgment require Secrecy; and the Yeas and Nays of the Members of either House on any question shall, at the Desire of one fifth of those Present, be entered on the Journal.

Neither House, during the Session of Congress, shall, without the Consent of the other, adjourn for more than three days, nor to any other Place than that in which the two Houses shall be sitting.

Section. 6. The Senators and Representatives shall receive a Compensation for their Services, to be ascertained by Law, and paid out of the Treasury of the United States. They shall in all Cases, except Treason, Felony and Breach of the Peace, be privileged from Arrest during their Attendance at the Session of their respective Houses, and in going to and returning from the same; and for any Speech or Debate in either House, they shall not be questioned in any other Place.

No Senator or Representative shall, during the Time for which he was elected, be appointed to any civil Office under the Authority of the United States, which shall have been created, or the Emoluments whereof shall have been increased during such time; and no Person holding any Office under the United States, shall be a Member of either House during his Continuance in Office.

Section. 7. All Bills for raising Revenue shall originate in the House of Representatives; but the Senate may propose or concur with Amendments as on other Bills.

Every Bill which shall have passed the House of Representatives and the Senate, shall, before it become a Law, be presented to the President of the

We the People of the United States,

in Order to **form** a more perfect **Union**, establish **Justice**, insure domestic **Tranquility**, provide for the common defence, promote the general **Welfare**, and secure the **Blessings** of **Liberty** to ourselves and our **Posterity**, do **ordain** and **establish** this Constitution for the United States of America.

FORM	WELFARE	ORDAIN
UNION	BLESSINGS	ESTABLISH
JUSTICE	LIBERTY	
TRANQUILITY	POSTERITY	

- TRIVIA WORD SEARCH -
(two words)

The Founding Fathers drafted the Constitution of the United States in 1787 to replace a prior founding document which had proven inadequate in providing a strong and effective national government.

What is the name of the document that was replaced?

_____

_____

EASY

```
N  C  O  B  X  U  T  L  Z  W  J  I  T  Q  V  Z  J  E
Y  Q  S  U  T  U  Y  J  T  M  G  S  S  B  K  B  L  I
Y  N  N  W  V  V  E  U  M  M  H  M  O  C  G  L  R  F
B  F  O  Q  A  C  I  S  H  K  S  A  H  R  D  D  O  A
W  R  R  I  S  I  Y  T  R  E  B  I  L  K  D  A  H  P
S  P  O  S  T  E  R  I  T  Y  M  C  V  E  R  A  S  T
A  W  Y  C  Y  A  C  C  R  Q  J  L  S  T  P  U  I  B
E  S  T  G  N  S  R  E  J  W  V  M  I  P  W  J  L  N
T  C  I  Z  O  A  W  E  D  M  Y  C  H  W  G  E  B  R
M  B  L  G  F  R  D  I  D  O  L  U  E  N  S  P  A  Z
N  O  I  N  U  D  X  L  B  E  P  L  I  S  B  B  T  C
M  G  U  W  S  V  Z  D  S  H  F  P  I  Y  R  J  S  Y
O  O  Q  O  J  Q  D  L  K  A  H  N  N  F  F  K  E  Y
D  K  N  Z  U  T  T  R  R  H  G  I  O  R  L  H  P  R
S  L  A  B  I  S  E  E  Q  S  U  R  K  C  K  N  I  H
C  W  R  N  T  K  K  G  T  S  M  H  Y  P  D  W  T  X
C  L  T  S  Q  M  L  R  P  H  Q  D  B  R  P  N  Z  D
D  Y  V  K  L  L  S  L  C  K  J  A  X  K  D  X  Q  O
```

EASY

LEGISLATIVE BRANCH

The legislative branch of the Constitution of the United States creates, debates, and enact laws that govern the country. It is comprised of two chambers, the Senate and the House of Representatives, which together form the United States Congress. The legislative branch represents the will of the people, levies taxes, regulates commerce, declares war, and ensures the checks and balances necessary to maintain a fair and functioning government.

ARTICLE. I

Section. 1.

All legislative **Powers** herein granted shall be **vested** in a **Congress** of the United States, which shall consist of a Senate and House of Representatives.

Section. 2.

The House of Representatives shall be **composed** of **Members chosen** every second Year by the People of the several States, and the Electors in each State shall have the Qualifications requisite for **Electors** of the most numerous Branch of the State Legislature.

No Person shall be a Representative who shall not have attained to the Age of twenty five Years, and been **seven Years** a **Citizen** of the United States, and who shall not, when elected, be an Inhabitant of that State in which he shall be chosen.

EASY

Representatives and direct **Taxes** shall be **apportioned among** the several States which may be included within this **Union**, according to their respective Numbers, which shall be determined by adding to the whole Number of free Persons, including those bound to Service for a Term of Years, and excluding Indians not taxed, three fifths of all other Persons.

The actual Enumeration shall be made within three Years after the first Meeting of the Congress of the United States, and within every subsequent Term of ten Years, in such Manner as they shall by Law direct. The Number of Representatives shall not exceed one for every thirty Thousand, but each **State** shall have at **Least one Representative**; and until such enumeration shall be made, the State of New Hampshire shall be entitled to chuse three, Massachusetts eight, Rhode-Island and Providence Plantations one, Connecticut five, New-York six, New Jersey four, Pennsylvania eight, Delaware one, Maryland six, Virginia ten, North Carolina five, South Carolina five, and Georgia three.

When vacancies happen in the Representation from any State, the Executive Authority thereof shall issue **Writs** of Election to **fill** such **Vacancies**.

The House of Representatives shall chuse their Speaker and other Officers; and shall have the sole Power of **Impeachment**.

EASY

(THE CONSTITUTION - ARTICLE I – LEGISLATIVE BRANCH)

POWERS	YEARS	ONE
VESTED	CITIZEN	REPRESENTATIVE
CONGRESS	TAXES	WRITS
COMPOSED	APPORTIONED	FILL
MEMBERS	AMONG	VACANCIES
CHOSEN	UNION	IMPEACHMENT
ELECTORS	STATE	
SEVEN	LEAST	

- TRIVIA WORD SEARCH -
(two words)

The purpose of the legislative branch of the Constitution of the United States is to create, debate, and pass laws. The legislative branch is responsible for representing the interests of the citizens, establishing national policies, and providing checks and balances on the other branches of government. It holds the power to levy taxes, regulate commerce, declare war, and manage the federal budget, among other responsibilities, ensuring a functioning and democratic government.

What two houses comprise the Legislative Branch?

_____

_____

EASY

```
B  H  C  M  U  T  N  E  M  H  C  A  E  P  M  I  O  J  Z  Y
Z  Q  N  A  Y  W  D  T  Y  F  I  V  K  S  J  W  Z  A  O  F
C  E  U  I  N  R  I  A  H  Z  H  X  C  A  U  A  A  O  G  I
F  P  T  V  D  I  C  T  U  Q  Y  D  E  S  O  P  M  O  C  L
V  P  V  A  E  T  R  S  B  X  F  C  V  X  P  P  R  S  M  L
G  R  J  I  N  S  L  E  C  J  S  L  Y  O  U  W  Y  Z  Q  Z
V  T  E  S  T  E  T  V  M  E  V  M  R  B  W  N  B  O  V  S
H  L  M  P  A  V  S  E  C  S  E  T  S  I  L  R  V  C  V  X
S  I  F  S  R  Z  Z  N  D  M  I  P  F  Y  E  A  R  S  V  N
E  R  T  V  K  E  X  M  B  O  P  V  C  L  C  S  R  D  T  F
I  R  E  P  R  E  S  E  N  T  A  T  I  V  E  S  O  X  T  R
C  S  E  W  P  H  R  E  I  G  Y  M  T  W  S  F  O  J  U  R
N  S  U  V  O  S  D  N  N  D  Y  M  I  S  R  Y  P  N  K  W
A  E  E  U  M  P  W  I  Q  T  G  M  Z  U  O  F  T  V  E  B
C  R  M  X  D  G  G  N  O  M  A  Z  E  R  T  F  M  P  J  O
A  G  X  W  A  X  A  B  M  C  D  T  N  P  C  K  S  O  B  R
V  N  P  A  H  T  I  Z  T  A  Z  E  I  R  E  B  M  A  L  F
C  O  M  T  O  U  C  S  K  M  G  P  R  V  L  N  U  Q  W  H
I  C  G  U  Q  E  F  X  A  A  P  E  P  N  E  S  O  H  C  K
O  D  M  G  O  K  O  L  G  O  Q  I  N  O  I  N  U  J  R  Q
```

EASY

Section. 3.

The Senate of the United States shall be composed of **two Senators** from each State, chosen by the Legislature thereof, for six Years; and **each** Senator shall have **one Vote**.

Immediately after they shall be assembled in Consequence of the first Election, they shall be **divided** as equally as may be into three **Classes**. The Seats of the Senators of the first Class shall be vacated at the Expiration of the second Year, of the second Class at the Expiration of the fourth Year, and of the third Class at the Expiration of the sixth Year, so that one third may be chosen every second Year; and if Vacancies happen by Resignation, or otherwise, during the Recess of the Legislature of any State, the Executive thereof may make temporary Appointments until the next Meeting of the Legislature, which shall then fill such Vacancies.

No Person shall be a Senator who shall not have attained to the **Age** of **thirty** Years, and been **nine** Years a **Citizen** of the United States, and who shall not, when elected, be an Inhabitant of that State for which he shall be chosen.

The **Vice President** of the United States shall be President of the Senate, but shall have no Vote, unless they be equally divided.

The Senate shall chuse their other Officers, and also a President **pro tempore**, in the **Absence** of the Vice President, or when he shall exercise the Office of President of the United States.

The Senate shall have the sole Power to try all Impeachments. When sitting for that Purpose, they shall be on Oath or Affirmation. When the President of the

EASY

United States is tried, the **Chief Justice** shall **preside**: And no Person shall be convicted without the Concurrence of two thirds of the Members present.

Judgment in Cases of **Impeachment** shall not extend further than to removal from Office, and disqualification to hold and enjoy any Office of honor, Trust or Profit under the United States: but the Party **convicted** shall nevertheless be **liable** and subject to Indictment, Trial, Judgment and Punishment, according to **Law**.

EASY

TWO	THIRTY	JUSTICE
SENATORS	NINE	PRESIDE
EACH	CITIZEN	IMPEACHMENT
ONE	VICE	CONVICTED
VOTE	PRESIDENT	LIABLE
DIVIDED	PRO	LAW
CLASSES	TEMPORE	
AGE	CHIEF	

- TRIVIA WORD SEARCH -
(two words)

Every two years, Senate members are elected (or reelected). The Constitution's framers based this system on precedents established by state governments.

What portion of the entire Senate Class is affected by these elections?.

_____

_____

EASY

```
M R D S V P V J R A U I R F T Q
E F V Q P P R Z S O W Y Y M O L
D B Q T K P R O E C G R M N S T
C N M W N R D Z S D W S E G A X
S A E R E E D I S E R P T J J T
H R N V D S M K A L V E H G U T
L L O I U I W H L V K Q I Y S S
Q T V T R D W M C W T G R C T G
E I J H A E J V M A D N D E I B
D U B C O N V I C T E D M L C G
H Y G O I T E Y W Q I P J B E F
T R K B V L B S T I O W M A E W
I W L C H I E F X R H Z A I A B
P B O Q H C C H E D I G H L C W
Y W H P X E R E N I N H S I H M
I X S C T J J U N E Z I T I C B
```

EASY

Section. 4.

The Times, Places and Manner of holding **Elections** for Senators and Representatives, shall be **prescribed** in each **State** by the **Legislature** thereof; but the Congress may at any time by Law make or alter such Regulations, except as to the Places of chusing Senators.

The **Congress** shall **assemble** at least **once** in every Year, and such Meeting shall be on the first Monday in December, unless they shall by Law appoint a different Day.

Section. 5.

Each House shall be the **Judge** of the Elections, Returns and Qualifications of its **own** Members, and a **Majority** of each shall constitute a **Quorum** to do Business; but a smaller Number may adjourn from day to day, and may be authorized to compel the Attendance of absent Members, in such Manner, and under such Penalties as each House may provide.

Each House may **determine** the **Rules** of its Proceedings, punish its Members for disorderly Behaviour, and, with the Concurrence of two thirds, expel a Member.

Each House shall **keep** a **Journal** of its Proceedings, and from time to time **publish** the same, excepting such Parts as may in their Judgment require Secrecy; and the Yeas and Nays of the Members of either House on any question shall, at the Desire of one fifth of those Present, be entered on the Journal.

EASY

Neither House, during the Session of Congress, shall, without the Consent of the other, adjourn for more than three days, nor to any other Place than that in which the two Houses shall be sitting.

Section. 6.

The Senators and Representatives shall receive a **Compensation** for their Services, to be ascertained by Law, and paid out of the Treasury of the United States. They shall in all Cases, except Treason, Felony and Breach of the Peace, be **privileged from Arrest** during their Attendance at the Session of their respective Houses, and in going to and returning from the same; and for any Speech or Debate in either House, they shall not be questioned in any other Place.

No Senator or Representative shall, during the Time for which he was elected, be appointed to any civil Office under the Authority of the United States, which shall have been created, or the Emoluments whereof shall have been encreased during such time; and no Person holding any Office under the United States, shall be a Member of either House during his Continuance in Office.

EASY

ELECTIONS	HOUSE	JOURNAL
PRESCRIBED	JUDGE	PUBLISH
STATE	OWN	COMPENSATION
LEGISLATURE	MAJORITY	PRIVILEDGED
CONGRESS	QUORUM	FROM
ASSEMBLE	DETERMINE	ARREST
ONCE	RULES	
EACH	KEEP	

- TRIVIA WORD SEARCH -
(two words)

Each house keeps a journal and publishes it periodically.

What information recorded requires approval from one-fifth of the House membership present before entering in the journal?

_____

_____

EASY

```
C T N E D E G D E L I V I R P T C
M A M F Z O R P S Y A N Q X E O S
B Y L I G K S U E J N O C S T J Y
I K E N I M R E T E D I J L R L G
M U R O U Q Q D Y A K T P K K E X
O J I O E G Y T Z H L A V D X Z C
E B A S P V I E Q A S S E M B L E
Y V U G M R S T A T E N I R M D S
R O M M O S E L U R L E S G N A J
H K L J R J I S N D E P C W E S A
Z O A R F U E A C H C M O Y T L T
H M N R W D R S X R T O N P D V N
U N R C R G O B H X I C G H E C Z
A A U B E E J L G T O B R F K Y A
A X O Q V X S F L C N Q E F U O Z
L E J V T C I T Q F S K S D J W O
W I L C Q K U P U B L I S H F R H
```

EASY

Section. 7.

All **Bills** for raising **Revenue** shall **originate** in the **House** of Representatives; but the Senate may propose or concur with Amendments as on other Bills.

Every Bill which shall have passed the House of Representatives and the Senate, shall, **before** it become a **Law**, be presented to the **President** of the United States; If he **approve** he shall sign it, but if not he shall **return** it, with his Objections to that House in which it shall have originated, who shall enter the Objections at large on their Journal, and proceed to **reconsider** it. If after such Reconsideration two thirds of that House shall agree to pass the Bill, it shall be sent, together with the **Objections**, to the other House, by which it shall likewise be reconsidered, and if approved by two thirds of that House, it shall become a Law. But in all such Cases the Votes of both Houses shall be determined by yeas and Nays, and the **Names** of the Persons voting for and against the Bill shall be **entered** on the **Journal** of each House respectively. If any Bill shall not be returned by the President within ten Days (Sundays excepted) after it shall have been presented to him, the Same shall be a Law, in like Manner as if he had signed it, unless the Congress by their Adjournment prevent its Return, in which Case it shall not be a Law.

Every Order, **Resolution**, or **Vote** to which the Concurrence of the Senate and House of Representatives may be necessary (except on a question of Adjournment) shall be presented to the President of the United States; and before the Same shall take Effect, shall be approved by him, or being disapproved by him, shall be **repassed** by **two thirds** of the Senate and House of Representatives, **according** to the **Rules** and Limitations **prescribed** in the Case of a Bill.

EASY

New Hampshire
(June 21, 1788)

Massachusetts

Massachusetts
(Feb 6, 1788)

New York
(July 26, 1788)

Rhode Island
(May 29, 1790)

unorg.
terr.

Connecticut
(January 9, 1788)

Pennsylvania
(December 12, 1787)

New Jersey
(December 18, 1787)

Connecticut

Delaware
(December 7, 1787)

Northwest
Territory

Maryland
(April 28, 1788)

Virginia
(July 26, 1788)

North
Carolina
(November 21, 1789)

South
Carolina
(May 23, 1788)

Georgia
(January 2, 1788)

THE CONSTITUTION
of the United States of America
Dates Ratified by the 13 States

EASY

BILLS	RETURN	VOTE
REVENUE	RECONSIDER	REPASSED
ORIGINATE	OBJECTIONS	TWO
HOUSE	NAMES	THIRDS
BEFORE	ENTERED	ACCORDING
LAW	JOURNAL	RULES
PRESIDENT	EVERY	
APPROVE	RESOLUTION	

- TRIVIA WORD SEARCH -
(one word)

What is the name of the Constitutional Right that the President has to unilaterally stop decisions made by Congress?

_____

EASY

```
K L R R I D E S S A P E R Z I
B B K D S S L A N R U O J V O
H O U S E G W H P R V B K I N
O W E L M J N E T P T E G H X
T T U A A S N I V H R F T M B
E R N W N T O S D O I O G O E
V F E E E W B C U R Z R V B D
T X V R R C J M J I O E D E E
P R E S I D E N T G O C G S K
L D R B U R C P S I S E C N P
R E S O L U T I O N I U Z A H
C V P S L L I B U A U W C O R
P E V Y G V O T E T L D U K I
L R E T U R N Y Q E D S G D T
K Y R E D I S N O C E R M G M
```

The Congress Shall Have Power To...

Section. 8.

The Congress shall have Power To lay and **collect Taxes**, Duties, Imposts and Excises, to **pay** the **Debts** and provide for the common Defence and general Welfare of the United States; but all Duties, Imposts and Excises shall be uniform throughout the United States;

To **borrow Money** on the credit of the United States;

To **regulate Commerce** with foreign Nations, and among the several States, and with the Indian Tribes;

To establish an uniform Rule of Naturalization, and uniform Laws on the subject of Bankruptcies throughout the United States;

To coin Money, regulate the Value thereof, and of foreign Coin, and fix the Standard of Weights and Measures;

To provide for the Punishment of counterfeiting the Securities and current Coin of the United States;

To establish **Post Offices** and post Roads;

To **promote** the Progress of **Science** and useful **Arts**, by securing for limited Times to Authors and Inventors the exclusive Right to their respective Writings and Discoveries;

To **constitute Tribunals** inferior to the supreme Court;

To define and punish Piracies and Felonies committed on the high Seas, and Offences against the Law of Nations;

EASY

To **declare War**, grant Letters of Marque and Reprisal, and make Rules concerning Captures on Land and Water;

To raise and support Armies, but no Appropriation of Money to that Use shall be for a longer Term than two Years;

To provide and maintain a Navy;

To make Rules for the Government and Regulation of the land and naval Forces;

To provide for calling forth the Militia to execute the Laws of the Union, **suppress Insurrections** and repel Invasions;

To provide for organizing, arming, and disciplining, the Militia, and for governing such Part of them as may be employed in the Service of the United States, reserving to the States respectively, the Appointment of the Officers, and the Authority of training the Militia according to the discipline prescribed by Congress;

To exercise exclusive **Legislation** in all Cases whatsoever, over such District (not exceeding ten Miles square) as may, by Cession of particular States, and the Acceptance of Congress, become the **Seat** of the **Government** of the United States, and to exercise like Authority over all Places purchased by the Consent of the Legislature of the State in which the Same shall be, for the Erection of Forts, Magazines, Arsenals, dock-Yards, and other needful Buildings;—And

To make all Laws which shall be necessary and proper for carrying into Execution the foregoing Powers, and all other Powers vested by this Constitution in the Government of the United States, or in any Department or Officer thereof.

EASY

COLLECT	POST	WAR
TAXES	OFFICES	SUPPRESS
PAY	PROMOTE	INSURRECTIONS
DEBTS	SCIENCE	LEGISLATION
BORROW	ARTS	SEAT
MONEY	CONSTITUTE	GOVERNMENT
REGULATE	TRIBUNALS	
COMMERCE	DECLARE	

- TRIVIA WORD SEARCH -
(two words)

What is the time limit on expenditures of monies for Armies raised and supported by Congress?

_____

_____

EASY

```
O  D  X  B  G  E  J  E  C  R  E  M  M  O  C  W  S  D
S  S  E  B  K  T  H  Z  F  A  E  S  O  Z  T  Q  Q  S
H  M  U  M  N  A  T  G  Y  Z  U  N  V  N  S  E  Y  G
N  V  C  E  K  L  I  S  J  Q  V  O  X  C  E  S  S  Z
P  P  I  N  S  U  R  R  E  C  T  I  O  N  S  Y  A  E
M  X  N  W  R  G  S  C  O  N  S  T  I  T  U  T  E  T
S  W  I  S  S  E  R  P  P  U  S  A  E  G  A  C  N  O
F  O  V  A  D  R  Q  Z  X  T  G  L  S  T  B  E  D  M
O  A  B  T  R  I  B  U  N  A  L  S  H  A  M  L  S  O
N  R  O  I  G  B  S  M  R  W  C  I  D  N  O  L  S  R
T  E  R  K  J  H  Y  E  A  R  S  G  R  W  P  O  W  P
N  O  R  R  Z  K  O  O  S  C  S  E  W  M  Z  C  O  H
E  W  O  A  E  Y  K  N  I  T  V  L  C  T  H  S  S  Y
J  T  W  W  L  E  F  E  A  O  R  N  K  I  T  H  O  Z
I  A  S  E  N  C  N  X  G  S  P  A  Y  L  F  Q  Z  S
S  W  P  Y  L  C  E  P  H  W  Y  Q  H  J  Y  F  E  X
X  L  L  U  E  S  G  D  B  A  B  S  S  U  G  C  O  V
F  J  N  Z  H  L  M  U  L  Z  H  T  P  E  B  G  V  P
```

EASY

Section. 9.

The Migration or **Importation** of such Persons as any of the States now existing shall think proper to admit, shall not be prohibited by the Congress prior to the Year one thousand eight hundred and eight, but a **Tax** or duty may be imposed on such Importation, not exceeding ten dollars for each Person.

The Privilege of the Writ of **Habeas Corpus** shall not be suspended, unless when in Cases of Rebellion or Invasion the public Safety may require it.

No **Bill** of **Attainder** or ex post facto Law shall be passed.

No **Capitation**, or other direct, Tax shall be laid, unless in Proportion to the Census or enumeration herein before directed to be taken.

No Tax or **Duty** shall be **laid** on Articles exported from any State.

No Preference shall be given by any **Regulation** of Commerce or Revenue to the Ports of one State over those of another: nor shall Vessels bound to, or from, one State, be obliged to enter, clear, or pay Duties in another.

No **Money** shall be drawn from the Treasury, but in Consequence of Appropriations made by Law; and a regular Statement and Account of the **Receipts** and Expenditures of all **public** Money shall be **published** from time to time.

No Title of Nobility shall be granted by the United States: And no Person holding any Office of Profit or **Trust** under them, shall, without the Consent of the Congress, accept of any present, Emolument, Office, or Title, of any kind whatever, from any King, Prince, or foreign State.

EASY

Section. 10.

No **State** shall enter into any Treaty, Alliance, or Confederation; grant Letters of Marque and Reprisal; coin Money; emit Bills of Credit; make any Thing but **gold** and **silver** Coin a Tender in Payment of Debts; pass any Bill of Attainder, ex post facto Law, or Law impairing the Obligation of Contracts, or grant any Title of Nobility.

No State shall, without the Consent of the Congress, lay any Imposts or Duties on Imports or Exports, except what may be absolutely necessary for executing it's inspection Laws: and the net Produce of all Duties and Imposts, laid by any State on **Imports** or **Exports**, shall be for the Use of the Treasury of the United States; and all such Laws shall be subject to the Revision and Controul of the **Congress**.

No State shall, without the **Consent** of Congress, lay any Duty of Tonnage, keep Troops, or Ships of War in time of Peace, enter into any Agreement or Compact with another State, or with a foreign Power, or engage in War, unless actually invaded, or in such imminent Danger as will not admit of delay.

EASY

IMPORTATION	LAID	GOLD
TAX	REGULATION	SILVER
HABEAS	MONEY	IMPORTS
CORPUS	RECEIPTS	EXPORTS
BILL	PUBLIC	CONGRESS
ATTAINDER	PUBLISHED	CONSENT
CAPITATION	TRUST	
DUTY	STATE	

- TRIVIA WORD SEARCH -
(two words)

Article I, Section 9 clause 8 (Foreign Emoluments Clause) assures that State and Federal Office Holders are not corrupted by foreign influences.

What specifically does this clause prohibit citizens of the United States from being granted?

_____

_____

EASY

```
I  R  G  I  E  M  D  M  S  Y  L  P  S  C  U  P
R  T  V  Y  S  T  B  O  U  G  A  U  T  O  W  Q
F  I  L  B  F  Y  S  N  P  O  N  B  R  N  R  D
A  T  T  A  I  N  D  E  R  L  O  L  O  G  I  L
Q  L  M  F  X  L  A  Y  O  D  I  I  P  R  M  P
Q  E  H  T  E  L  L  B  C  M  T  S  M  E  V  I
E  I  Q  C  Y  C  H  F  P  A  A  H  I  S  H  Z
S  T  R  O  P  X  E  O  L  E  T  E  K  S  V  C
Q  F  A  E  B  S  R  U  B  C  I  D  K  O  C  Z
C  U  R  I  C  T  G  A  C  R  P  T  Y  V  T  S
O  X  T  B  A  E  H  B  E  V  A  K  U  J  S  I
N  Q  G  T  R  M  I  V  R  X  C  A  R  D  U  Y
S  L  I  G  D  G  L  P  U  B  L  I  C  I  R  Z
E  O  N  O  B  I  L  I  T  Y  Z  S  T  A  T  E
N  F  P  H  S  I  C  E  S  S  W  C  G  L  B  I
T  A  G  Y  T  U  D  B  Y  Z  N  Q  O  R  G  D
```

EASY

EXECUTIVE BRANCH

The executive branch of the Constitution of the United States enforces and implements federal laws and policies. Headed by the President, the executive branch includes the Vice President and the President's Cabinet, along with various federal agencies and departments. The President serves as the Commander-in-Chief of the armed forces, negotiates treaties, appoints federal officials and judges, and ensures that laws passed by Congress are faithfully executed. This branch is essential for the day-to-day administration and operation of the federal government.

ARTICLE. II

Section. 1.

The **executive** Power shall be vested in a President of the United States of America. He shall hold his Office during the Term of four Years, and, together with the Vice President, chosen for the same Term, be elected, as follows

Each State shall appoint, in such Manner as the Legislature thereof may direct, a Number of Electors, equal to the whole Number of Senators and Representatives to which the State may be entitled in the Congress: but no Senator or Representative, or **Person** holding an Office of Trust or Profit under the United States, shall be appointed an Elector.

The Electors shall meet in their respective States, and vote by Ballot for two Persons, of whom one at least shall not be an Inhabitant of the same State with themselves. And they shall make a List of all the Persons voted for, and of the

MEDIUM

Number of Votes for each; which List they shall sign and certify, and transmit sealed to the Seat of the Government of the United States, directed to the President of the Senate. The President of the Senate shall, in the Presence of the Senate and House of Representatives, open all the Certificates, and the Votes shall then be counted. The Person having the greatest Number of Votes shall be the President, if such Number be a Majority of the whole Number of Electors appointed; and if there be more than one who have such Majority, and have an equal Number of Votes, then the House of Representatives shall immediately **chuse** by Ballot one of them for President; and if no Person have a Majority, then from the five highest on the List the said House shall in like Manner chuse the President. But in chusing the President, the Votes shall be taken by States, the Representation from each State having one Vote; A quorum for this Purpose shall consist of a Member or Members from two thirds of the States, and a Majority of all the States shall be necessary to a Choice. In every Case, after the Choice of the President, the Person having the greatest Number of Votes of the Electors shall be the Vice President. But if there should remain two or more who have equal Votes, the Senate shall chuse from them by Ballot the Vice President.

The Congress may determine the Time of chusing the Electors, and the Day on which they shall give their Votes; which Day shall be the **same** throughout the United States.

No Person except a **natural** born **Citizen**, or a Citizen of the United States, at the time of the Adoption of this Constitution, shall be eligible to the Office of President; neither shall any Person be eligible to that Office who shall not have

MEDIUM

attained to the **Age** of thirty five **Years**, and been fourteen Years a Resident within the United States.

In Case of the Removal of the President from Office, or of his Death, Resignation, or Inability to discharge the Powers and Duties of the said Office, the Same shall devolve on the Vice President, and the Congress may by Law provide for the Case of Removal, Death, Resignation or Inability, both of the President and Vice President, declaring what Officer shall then act as President, and such Officer shall act accordingly, until the Disability be removed, or a President shall be elected.

The President shall, at stated Times, receive for his Services, a Compensation, which shall neither be **encreased** nor diminished during the Period for which he shall have been elected, and he shall not receive within that Period any other Emolument from the United States, or any of them.

Before he enter on the Execution of his Office, he shall take the following Oath or **Affirmation**:—"I do solemnly swear (or affirm) that I will faithfully execute the Office of President of the United States, and will to the best of my Ability, preserve, protect and defend the Constitution of the United States."

MEDIUM

I do SOLEMNLY SWEAR (or affirm) that

I will FAITHFULLY EXECUTE

the

OFFICE OF PRESIDENT

of the United States.

and WILL to the best of my ability,

PRESERVE, PROTECT and DEFEND

THE CONSTITUTION

of the United States.

MEDIUM

Answer the following questions to reveal a word from the preceding exert. Next, find the word in the puzzle.

1. What power is vested in the President of the United States? (1 word)

_____

2. Who elects the President and Vice President of the United States? (1 word)

_____

3. Who cannot be appointed as an elector? (3 words)

_____

_____

4. On what day do the electors give their votes? (1 word)

_____

5. What are the three eligibility requirements to be President? (8 words)

_____

_____

6. Who assumes the presidency if the President is removed from office, dies, resigns, or is unable to discharge the powers and duties of the office? (2 words)

_____

7. What stipulations are placed upon the compensation that the President receives? (3 words)

_____

8. What must the President take before entering the execution of his office? (2 words)

_____

9. Who sets the time of choosing the electors and the day on which they give their votes? (1 word)

_____

10. What act must the House of Representatives do if there is a tie in the electoral vote for President? (1 word)

_____

11. What is the President required to protect and defend when being sworn in to office of the Presidency? (1 word)

_____

MEDIUM

```
E  C  N  U  G  S  K  J  H  E  D  B  U  R  W  U  F  W  U  Z
F  G  F  A  K  T  A  U  F  R  S  N  G  E  M  O  R  C  H  K
B  V  S  I  O  V  V  M  V  R  B  M  P  O  A  V  B  O  R  N
B  K  E  E  U  S  I  L  E  M  J  K  B  A  Z  K  G  N  Q  L
O  P  D  R  V  O  O  C  N  L  O  S  M  A  T  S  T  G  A  E
X  E  G  A  O  I  A  N  E  F  T  N  E  D  I  S  E  R  L  S
A  B  I  W  D  U  T  W  Z  G  O  Z  N  N  G  G  U  E  X  M
O  Y  T  D  Q  L  H  A  I  I  L  R  C  S  A  T  C  S  F  C
H  A  F  F  I  R  M  A  T  I  O  N  R  H  A  T  I  S  T  T
M  N  D  M  X  M  D  U  I  N  B  A  E  N  O  G  O  J  P  J
F  S  C  E  S  P  T  I  C  F  E  A  A  R  P  O  G  R  E  M
B  F  N  M  X  I  I  T  M  Y  H  S  S  R  U  P  S  M  S  G
F  O  U  O  T  E  R  Z  I  I  C  C  E  W  W  U  F  E  V  Y
M  Z  W  S  S  O  C  J  R  A  N  S  D  R  E  O  I  D  K  H
I  G  N  H  K  R  D  U  N  P  I  I  V  H  P  X  V  U  D  Z
C  O  V  N  P  A  E  N  T  D  C  N  S  R  O  E  E  E  M  F
C  C  L  B  E  E  O  P  E  I  U  J  X  H  V  B  R  R  T  K
Y  T  R  I  H  T  K  N  T  P  V  Q  W  A  E  N  N  K  A  I
R  A  Z  F  T  C  T  E  N  G  B  E  U  X  S  D  B  I  M  X
V  V  J  E  X  A  G  K  G  W  B  U  L  B  A  A  U  V  S  Z
```

MEDIUM

Section. 2.

The President shall be Commander in Chief of the Army and Navy of the United States, and of the Militia of the several States, when called into the actual Service of the United States; he may require the Opinion, in writing, of the principal Officer in each of the executive Departments, upon any Subject relating to the Duties of their respective Offices, and he shall have Power to grant Reprieves and Pardons for Offences against the United States, except in Cases of Impeachment.

He shall have Power, by and with the Advice and Consent of the **Senate**, to make Treaties, provided two thirds of the Senators present concur; and he shall nominate, and by and with the Advice and Consent of the Senate, shall appoint Ambassadors, other public Ministers and Consuls, Judges of the supreme Court, and all other **Officers** of the United States, whose Appointments are not herein otherwise provided for, and which shall be established by Law: but the Congress may by Law vest the Appointment of such inferior Officers, as they think proper, in the President alone, in the Courts of Law, or in the Heads of Departments.

The President shall have Power to fill up all Vacancies that may happen during the Recess of the Senate, by granting Commissions which shall **expire** at the End of their next Session.

Section. 3.

He shall from time to time give to the Congress Information of the **State** of the Union, and recommend to their Consideration such Measures as he shall judge necessary and expedient; he may, on extraordinary Occasions, convene both Houses, or either of them, and in Case of Disagreement between them, with Respect to the Time of Adjournment, he may adjourn them to such Time as he shall think proper; he shall receive Ambassadors and other public Ministers; he

MEDIUM

shall take Care that the Laws be faithfully executed, and shall **Commission** all the Officers of the United States.

Section. 4.

The President, Vice President and all civil Officers of the United States, shall be removed from Office on **Impeachment** for, and Conviction of, Treason, Bribery, or other high Crimes and Misdemeanors.

MEDIUM

1. In addition to the Army and Navy, over which other forces does the President serve as Commander in Chief? (1 word)

2. What power does the President have to grant for offenses against the United States, except in cases of impeachment? (2 words)

3. With whose advice and consent does the President have the power to make treaties? (1 word)

4. What fraction of the Senators present must concur for a treaty to be made? (2 words)

5. Whom does the President have the power to appoint with the advice and consent of the Senate? (5 words)

6. What power does the President have to fill vacancies that happen during the recess of the Senate? (5 words)

7. What annual message is the President required to give to Congress? (2 words)

8. On what type of occasions can the President convene both Houses of Congress? (1 word)

9. What must the President ensure about the laws? (2 words)

10. What can the President do to officers of the United States? (1 word)

11. What two things must occur to lead to the removal of the President, Vice President, and all civil officers from office? (2 words)

MEDIUM

```
D Z X X J Z L L P O U O P S Y G I V
Y M D D P D R G P A R D O N S F B M
T H S G M M D E N M C M X X S Q K T
T G H R G I L V B B F A O O I Y A Z
O N Z E E T A T S A S X C L P M I B
B I E D X C Z L R S D V J S O W T U
E T X M S T I J L S R E T S I N I M
W N N I H N R F F A I T H F U L L Y
I A M O O C O A F D H E L O S U I F
L R P I I D A I O O T S H E L H M O
E G N C C T L E S R U V V I W N D L
T U Z Y G J C U P S D E H Z D M O B
A N C Y U A G I Q M I I R R G U L A
N T F D L D Q A V R I M N I S Y C F
E S G B F P B T P N E Z M A P S F L
S E X E C U T E D X O Y F O R X V T
S B T P S O R N W H I C H H C Y E Y
C B C L E S L U S N O C O R I A B Y
```

MEDIUM

JUDICIAL BRANCH

The judicial branch of the Constitution of the United States interprets and applies the law, ensuring justice is administered fairly and consistently. Headed by the Supreme Court, this branch includes lower federal courts and is responsible for reviewing the constitutionality of laws, resolving legal disputes, and protecting individual rights. By providing checks and balances on the legislative and executive branches, the judicial branch helps maintain the rule of law and uphold the principles of the Constitution.

ARTICLE. III

Section. 1.

The judicial Power of the United States, shall be vested in one supreme Court, and in such inferior Courts as the Congress may from time to time ordain and establish. The Judges, both of the supreme and inferior Courts, shall hold their Offices during good Behaviour, and shall, at stated Times, receive for their Services, a Compensation, which shall not be diminished during their Continuance in Office.

Section. 2.

The judicial Power shall extend to all Cases, in Law and Equity, arising under this **Constitution**, the **Laws** of the United States, and **Treaties** made, or which shall be made, under their Authority;—to all Cases affecting Ambassadors, other public Ministers and Consuls;—to all Cases of admiralty and maritime Jurisdiction;—to Controversies to which the United States shall be a Party;—to Controversies between two or more States;— between a State and Citizens of another State,—between Citizens of different States,—between Citizens of the

MEDIUM

same State claiming Lands under Grants of different States, and between a State, or the Citizens thereof, and foreign States, Citizens or Subjects.

In all Cases affecting Ambassadors, other public Ministers and Consuls, and those in which a State shall be Party, the supreme Court shall have original Jurisdiction. In all the other Cases before mentioned, the supreme Court shall have appellate Jurisdiction, both as to Law and Fact, with such Exceptions, and under such Regulations as the Congress shall make.

The Trial of all Crimes, except in Cases of Impeachment, shall be by Jury; and such Trial shall be held in the State where the said Crimes shall have been **committed**; but when not committed within any State, the Trial shall be at such Place or Places as the Congress may by Law have directed.

Section. 3.

Treason against the United States, shall consist only in levying War against them, or in **adhering** to their Enemies, **giving** them Aid and Comfort. No Person shall be convicted of Treason unless on the Testimony of two Witnesses to the same overt Act, or on Confession in open Court.

The Congress shall have Power to declare the Punishment of Treason, but no Attainder of Treason shall work Corruption of Blood, or Forfeiture except during the Life of the Person attainted.

MEDIUM

1. What power is vested in the Supreme Court? (1 word)

2. What is required for judges of the Supreme and inferior courts to hold their offices? (2 word)

3. What cannot be diminished during a judge's continuance in office? (1 word)

4. What types of cases does the judicial power extend to? (3 words)

5. Which article and section outline that the judicial power extends to controversies between two or more states? (2 words)

6. In all other cases before mentioned, what type of jurisdiction does the Supreme Court have? (2 words)

7. How must the Trial of all Crimes be conducted? (1 word)

8. Where shall trials of all crimes, except in cases of impeachment, be held? (2 words)

9. In addition to levying war, what defines the crime of treason against the United States in regards to its enemies? (4 words)

10. What is required for a person to be convicted of treason? (2 words)

11. Who has the power to declare the punishment of treason? (1 word)

12. What length of restriction is placed on the punishment of treason regarding "corruption of blood" or forfeiture?(1 word)

13. By what mechanisms does the judicial branch maintain the rule of law and uphold the principles of the Constitution. (2 words)

MEDIUM

```
Z H I N O I T C I D S I R U J Q D
A E N B A L A N C E S P N G I F L
Z M S O I D S W S X R J O Z S O R
D K R Y I A H E H Q W G I D M J S
N G H P R T S E E I D I T E O C S
Z J L A W S A M R B V V U T F O T
D W X S E H I S E I G I T T W I G
T P R N E T D H N P N N I I H H L
X P T T R E A T I E S G T M T N Z
G I I J B V L K S P H S M R N L
W J U D I C I A L S Q M N O O M P
Q R Q O N O I S S E F N O C F X S
Y G R H R D J Z E P W C C M N O
L P X Q N Q O R A G T P I E O R A
D B Y Y I G H F E N R S A G C J L
Z Q S T A T E D K O R W D N A G
I U I U X Q R S K C E H C U Z F U
```

MEDIUM

STATES

Article IV establishes the framework for cooperation and respectful interaction among states, as well as delineating the responsibilities of the federal government in maintaining unity and stability among them.

ARTICLE. IV

Section. 1.

Full Faith and Credit shall be given in each State to the public Acts, Records, and judicial Proceedings of every other State. And the Congress may by general Laws prescribe the Manner in which such Acts, Records and Proceedings shall be proved, and the Effect thereof.

Section. 2.

The Citizens of each State shall be entitled to all Privileges and Immunities of Citizens in the several States.

A Person charged in any State with Treason, Felony, or other Crime, who shall flee from **Justice**, and be found in another State, shall on Demand of the executive Authority of the State from which he fled, be delivered up, to be removed to the State having Jurisdiction of the Crime.

No Person held to Service or Labour in one State, under the Laws thereof, escaping into another, shall, in Consequence of any Law or Regulation therein, be discharged from such Service or Labour, but shall be delivered up on Claim of the Party to whom such Service or Labour may be due.

Section. 3.

HARD

New States may be admitted by the Congress into this Union; but no new State shall be formed or erected within the **Jurisdiction** of any other State; nor any State be formed by the Junction of two or more States, or Parts of States, without the Consent of the Legislatures of the States concerned as well as of the Congress.

The Congress shall have Power to dispose of and make all needful **Rules** and **Regulations** respecting the Territory or other Property belonging to the United States; and nothing in this Constitution shall be so construed as to Prejudice any Claims of the United States, or of any particular State.

Section. 4.

The United States shall guarantee to every State in this Union a Republican Form of Government, and shall protect each of them against Invasion; and on Application of the Legislature, or of the Executive (when the Legislature cannot be convened) against domestic Violence.

HARD

(THE CONSTITUTION - ARTICLE IV – THE STATES)

Unscramble the following words to reveal a word from the preceding exert.
Next, find the word in the puzzle.

1. **RYTRIOTER**
2. **NEYOFL**
3. **IGIVPSEREL**
4. **SREUL**
5. **CORINDIJTIUS**
6. **TOYRREPP**
7. **HITAF**
8. **NEOSCTN**
9. **EUECIDRJP**
10. **JCSEIUT**
11. **NUERAGTEA**
12. **SNEORAT**
13. **RTSOLAEIUNG**
14. **EGPCASNI**
15. **TADEITDM**
16. **RDCSREO**
17. **LUEPNRICAB**
18. **ISIMNUIMTE**
19. **UJCNIONT**
20. **MERIC**

HARD

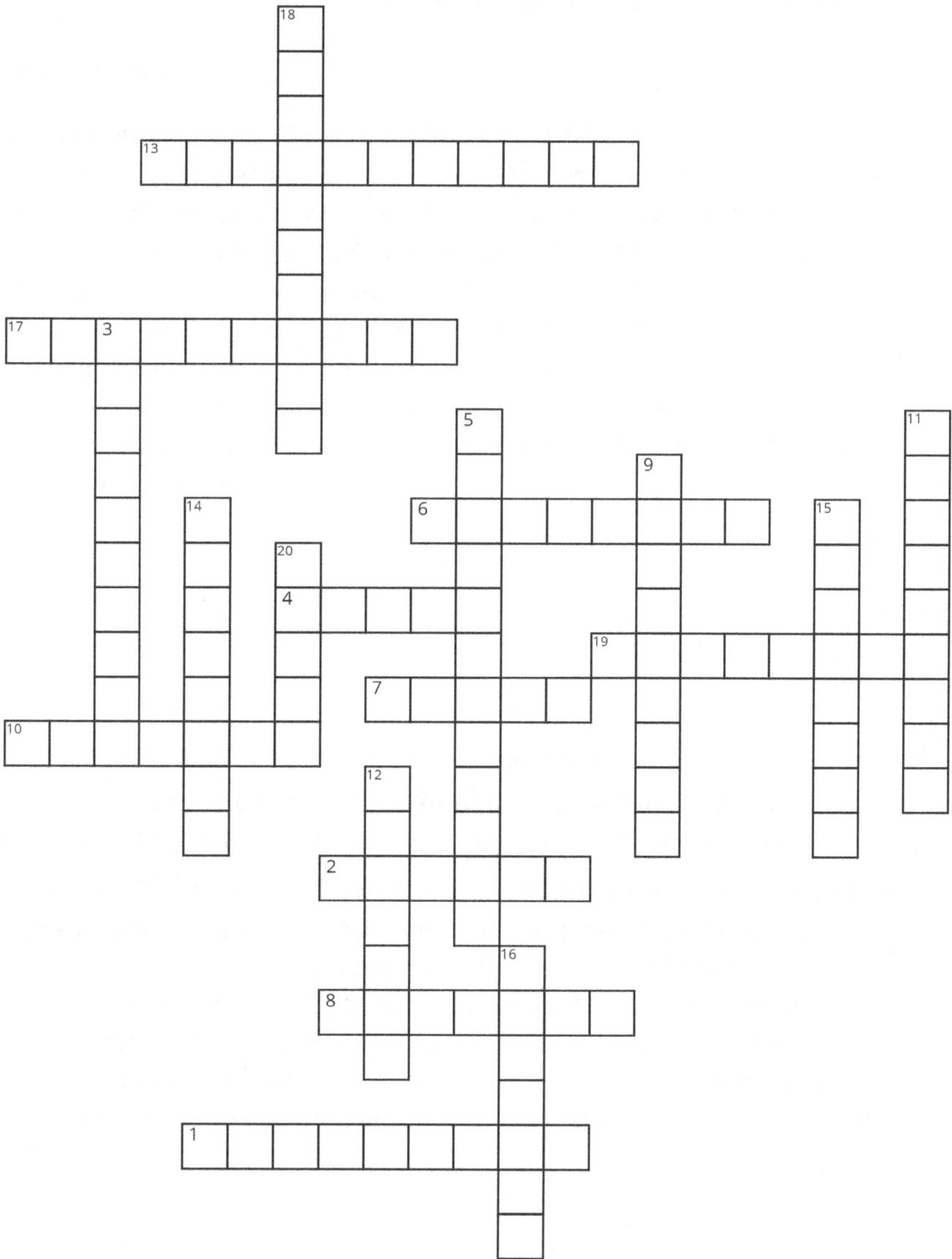

HARD

AMENDMENTS

Article V of the Constitution of the USA explains how the Constitution can be changed or amended. It sets out the process for making these changes, ensuring that the Constitution can be updated as needed. The process involves proposing an amendment, either by a two-thirds vote in both houses of Congress or by a national convention called by two-thirds of state legislatures. The proposed amendment then must be approved by three-fourths of the state legislatures or state conventions. This process ensures that changes to the Constitution are carefully considered and widely agreed upon.

ARTICLE. V

The Congress, whenever two thirds of both Houses shall deem it necessary, shall propose Amendments to this Constitution, or, on the Application of the Legislatures of two thirds of the several **States**, shall call a Convention for proposing Amendments, which, in either Case, shall be valid to all Intents and Purposes, as Part of this Constitution, when ratified by the **Legislatures** of three fourths of the several States, or by Conventions in three fourths thereof, as the one or the other Mode of Ratification may be proposed by the Congress; Provided that no Amendment which may be made prior to the Year One thousand eight hundred and eight shall in any Manner affect the first and fourth Clauses in the Ninth Section of the first Article; and that no State, without its Consent, shall be deprived of its equal Suffrage in the Senate.

HARD

U.S. HOUSE OF REPRESENTATIVES
(Seats by State)

The number of seats allocated to each state changes based on the population of the state. The total number of seats however is fixed at 435.

Shade the squares to indicate the party for each seat within the states!

HARD

Unscramble the following words to reveal a word from the preceding exert.
Next, find the word in the puzzle.

1. EVHNREWE
2. RUFGSAEF
3. DIALV
4. MNESTANDEM
5. NONOENITVC
6. DANUSHOT
7. SHUESO
8. AETENS
9. IPEDDVRE
10. SETRISLAEULG
11. YSECERASN
12. MRNENA
13. ATSEST
14. RPPOOES
15. ARIOIFACTINT
16. NITSENT
17. RSUPESPO
18. NLPIACOITPA
19. USLSAEC
20. ASELREV

HARD

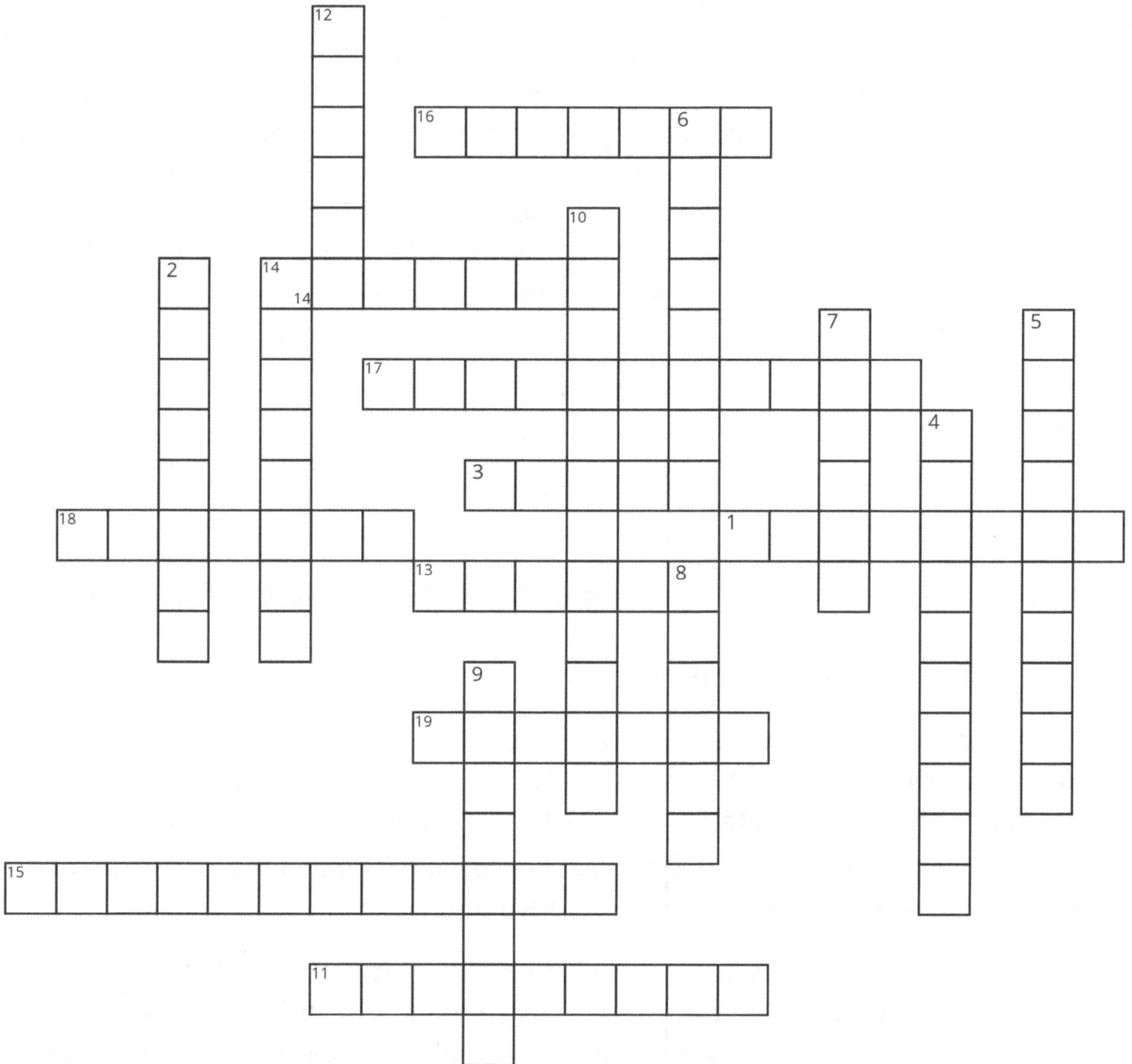

HARD

DEBTS, SUPREMACY, OATHS

Article VI ensures that laws and treaties made by the Federal Government are supreme to those made by the states. It also requires that all federal and state officials take an oath to support the Constitution, ensuring their loyalty to the nation's highest legal document. The clause also explicitly establishes that religion can never be used as a test to qualify anyone for a position of trust or office under the United States. And, established that all debts incurred by the nation prior to the adoption of the Constitution would be honored and paid.

ARTICLE. VI

All **Debts** contracted and Engagements entered into, before the Adoption of this Constitution, shall be as valid against the United States under this Constitution, as under the Confederation.

This Constitution, and the Laws of the United States which shall be made in Pursuance thereof; and all Treaties made, or which shall be made, under the Authority of the United States, shall be the supreme Law of the Land; and the Judges in every State shall be **bound** thereby, any Thing in the Constitution or Laws of any State to the Contrary notwithstanding.

The Senators and Representatives before mentioned, and the Members of the several State Legislatures, and all executive and judicial Officers, both of the United States and of the several States, shall be bound by Oath or Affirmation, to support this Constitution; but no religious Test shall ever be required as a Qualification to any Office or public **Trust** under the United States.

HARD

I do SOLEMNLY SWEAR that I will SUPPORT and DEFEND the CONSTITUTION of the united states against all enemies, foreign and domestic: that I WILL BEAR true FAITH and ALLEGIANCE to the same: that I take this obligation FREELY, WITHOUT any mental RESERVATION or purpose of evasion: and that I WILL well and faithfully DISCHARGE the DUTIES of the OFFICE on which I am about to enter: SO HELP ME GOD.

HARD

Unscramble the following words to reveal a word from the preceding exert. Next, find the word in the puzzle.

1. **AURSUPENC**

2. **SFCIFREO**

3. **ARYIOUHTT**

4. **IDAVL**

5. **RSLUIGOIE**

6. **UOBDN**

7. **EMRESMB**

8. **EDBST**

9. **FAFINAMOTIR**

10. **SREIATET**

11. **NSAIAGT**

12. **EUEVXCTIE**

13. **ODTOPINA**

14. **TURTSS**

15. **MEURPSE**

16. **YCRNOTRA**

17. **SNATGEMNEGE**

18. **RDEURIEQ**

19. **OCNTEEDRAIFON**

20. **DONEIENTM**

HARD

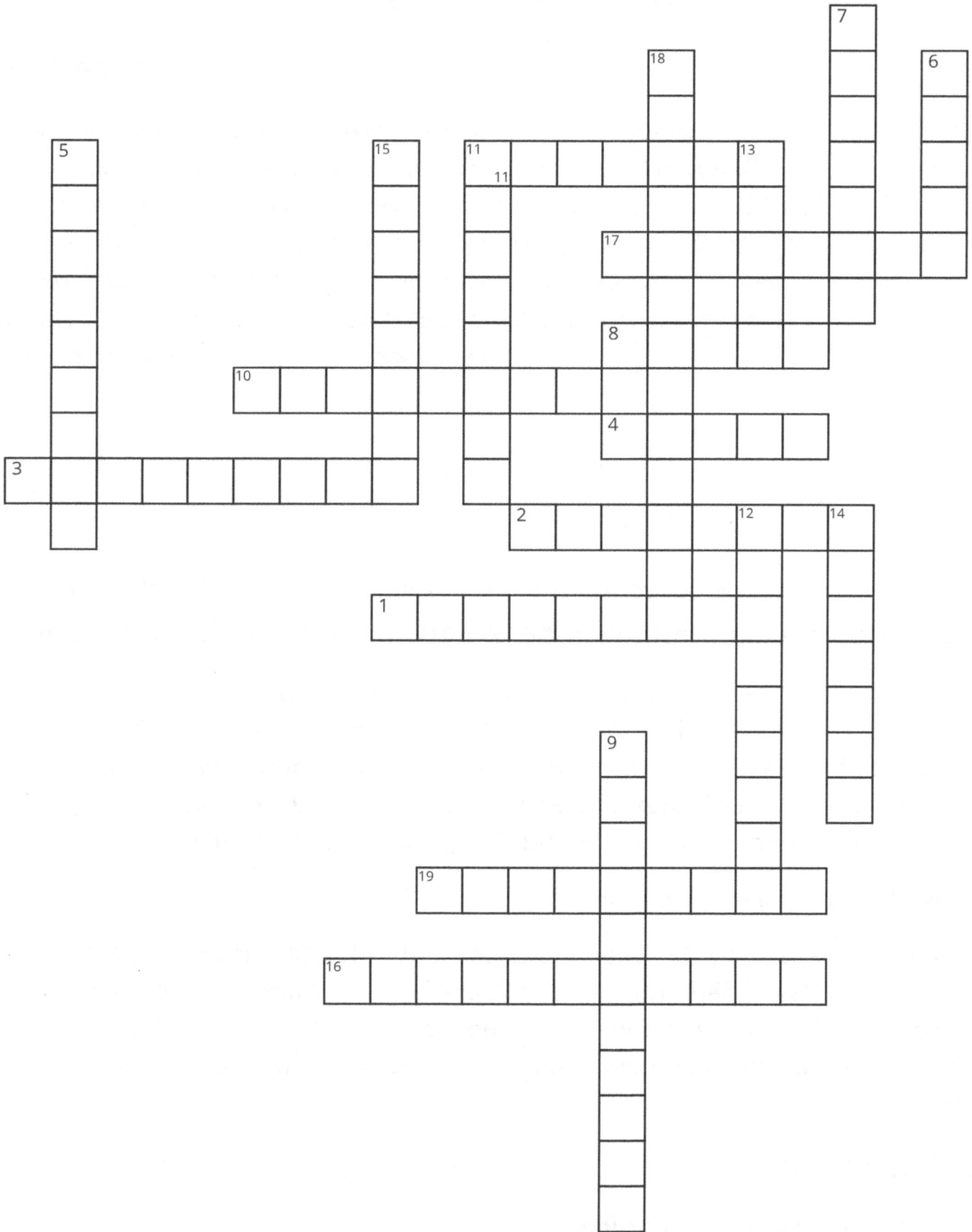

HARD

RATIFICATION

This article outlines the process for ratifying, or officially approving, the Constitution. It specifies that the Constitution would take effect once it was ratified by nine of the thirteen original states. Article VII was essential for transitioning from the Articles of Confederation to the new framework of government established by the Constitution, ensuring that there was sufficient support among the states for this significant change.

ARTICLE. VII

The Ratification of the Conventions of nine States, shall be sufficient for the Establishment of this Constitution **between** the States so ratifying the Same.

The Word, "the," being interlined between the seventh and eighth Lines of the first Page, The Word "Thirty" being partly written on an Erazure in the fifteenth Line of the first Page, The Words "is tried" being interlined between the thirty second and thirty third Lines of the first Page and the Word "the" being interlined between the forty third and forty fourth Lines of the second Page.

Attest William Jackson Secretary

done in Convention by the Unanimous Consent of the States present the Seventeenth Day of September in the Year of our Lord one thousand seven hundred and Eighty seven and of the Independance of the United States of America the Twelfth In witness whereof We have hereunto subscribed our Names,

G. **Washington**

Presidt and deputy from Virginia

HARD

SIGNERS

Delaware

George Read

Gunning Bedford Jr.

John Dickinson

Richard Bassett

Jacob Broom

Maryland

James McHenry

Daniel of St. Thomas Jenifer

Daniel Carroll

Virginia

George Washington

John Blair

James Madison

North Carolina

William Blount

Richard Dobbs Spaight

Hugh **Williamson**

South Carolina

John Rutledge

Charles Cotesworth Pinckney

Charles Pinckney

Pierce Butler

Georgia

William Few

Abraham Baldwin

New Hampshire

John Langdon

Nicholas Gilman

Massachusetts

Nathaniel Gorham

Rufus King

Connecticut

William Samuel Johnson

Roger Sherman

New York

Alexander **Hamilton**

New Jersey

William Livingston

David Brearley

William Paterson

Jonathan Dayton

Pennsylvania

Benjamin Franklin

Thomas Mifflin

Robert Morris

George Clymer

Thomas FitzSimons

Jared Ingersoll

James Wilson

Gouverneur Morris

HARD

(THE CONSTITUTION - ARTICLE VII – RATIFICATION)

Unscramble the following words to reveal a word from the preceding exert.
Next, find the word in the puzzle.

1. **TAHNSIGWNO**

2. **NSUIUMONA**

3. **OMLNIAISWL**

4. **WENTEBE**

5. **MONLAITH**

6. **EENTRLIDN**

7. **REESNPT**

8. **INIKNSODC**

9. **TFENSICINUF**

10. **SWINTES**

11. **GLITINVNSO**

12. **SNONCET**

13. **IRYTIFAGN**

14. **MPRETEEBS**

15. **DAMINSO**

16. **TSTAET**

17. **INSWOL**

18. **KRNINALFI**

19. **OCNSITONEVN**

20. **EYERTCARS**

HARD

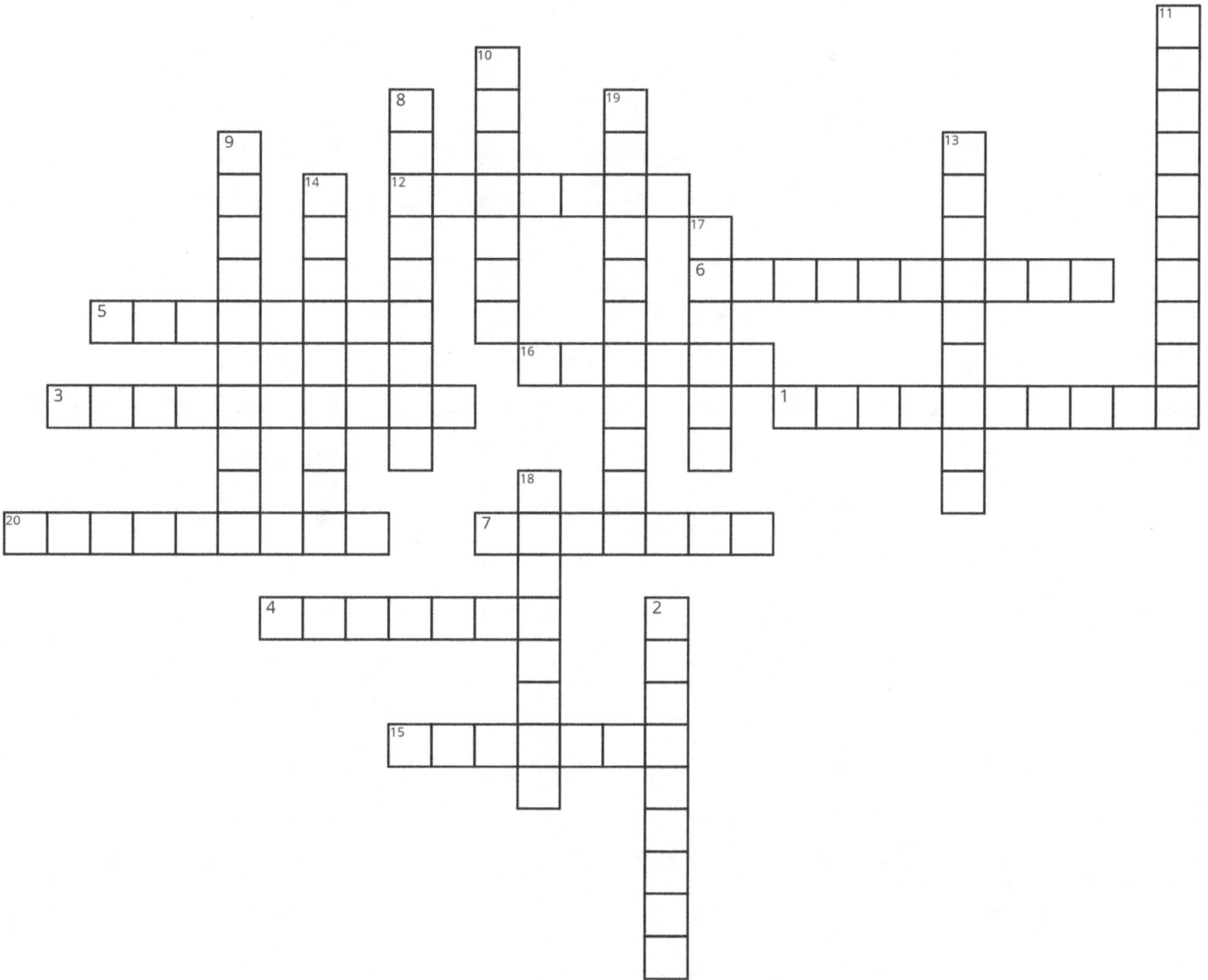

HARD

THE BILL OF RIGHTS

RATIFIED

December 15, 1791

PURPOSE

Defines Americans' rights in relation to their government. It guarantees an individual's civil rights and liberties. It also specifies that "the enumeration in the Constitution, of certain rights, shall not be construed to deny or disparage others retained by the people."

SIGNATORIES

President Washington sent copies to each State to be Ratified.

Congrefs of the United States,

begun and held at the City of New-York, on

Wednesday the fourth of March, one thousand, seven hundred and eighty-nine.

THE Conventions of a number of the States, having at the time of their adopting the Constitution, expressed a desire, in order to prevent misconstruction or abuse of its powers, that further declaratory and restrictive clauses should be added: And as extending the ground of public confidence in the Government, will best ensure the beneficent ends of its institution.

RESOLVED by the Senate and House of Representatives of the United States of America, in Congress assembled, two thirds of both Houses concurring, that the following Articles be proposed to the Legislatures of the several States, as amendments to the Constitution of the United States, all, or any of which Articles, when ratified by three fourths of the said Legislatures, to be valid to all intents and purposes, as part of the said Constitution; viz.

ARTICLES in addition to, and amendment of the Constitution of the United States of America, proposed by Congress, and ratified by the Legislatures of the several States, pursuant to the fifth Article of the original Constitution.

Article the first. After the first enumeration required by the first Article of the Constitution, there shall be one Representative for every thirty thousand, until the number shall amount to one hundred, after which the proportion shall be so regulated by Congress, that there shall be not less than one hundred Representatives, nor less than one Representative for every forty thousand persons, until the number of Representatives shall amount to two hundred, after which the proportion shall be so regulated by Congress, that there shall not be less than two hundred Representatives, nor more than one Representative for every fifty thousand persons.

Article the second. No law, varying the compensation for the services of the Senators and Representatives, shall take effect, until an election of Representatives shall have intervened.

Article the third. Congress shall make no law respecting an establishment of religion, or prohibiting the free exercise thereof; or abridging the freedom of speech, or of the press; or the right of the people peaceably to assemble, and to petition the Government for a redress of grievances.

Article the fourth. A well regulated militia, being necessary to the security of a free State, the right of the people to keep and bear arms, shall not be infringed.

Article the fifth. No soldier shall, in time of peace be quartered in any house, without the consent of the owner, nor in time of war, but in a manner to be prescribed by law.

Article the sixth. The right of the people to be secure in their persons, houses, papers, and effects, against unreasonable searches and seizures, shall not be violated, and no warrants shall issue, but upon probable cause, supported by oath or affirmation, and particularly describing the place to be searched, and the persons or things to be seized.

Article the seventh. No person shall be held to answer for a capital, or otherwise infamous crime, unless on a presentment or indictment of a grand jury, except in cases arising in the land or naval forces, or in the militia, when in actual service in time of war or public danger; nor shall any person be subject for the same offence to be twice put in jeopardy of life or limb; nor shall be compelled in any criminal case to be a witness against himself, nor be deprived of life, liberty, or property, without due process of law; nor shall private property be taken for public use, without just compensation.

Article the eighth. In all criminal prosecutions, the accused shall enjoy the right to a speedy and public trial, by an impartial jury of the State and district wherein the crime shall have been committed, which district shall have been previously ascertained by law, and to be informed of the nature and cause of the accusation; to be confronted with the witnesses against him; to have compulsory process for obtaining witnesses in his favor, and to have the assistance of counsel for his defence.

Article the ninth. In suits at common law, where the value in controversy shall exceed twenty dollars, the right of trial by jury shall be preserved, and no fact tried by a jury, shall be otherwise re-examined in any Court of the United States, than according to the rules of the common law.

Article the tenth. Excessive bail shall not be required, nor excessive fines imposed, nor cruel and unusual punishments inflicted.

Article the eleventh. The enumeration in the Constitution, of certain rights, shall not be construed to deny or disparage others retained by the people.

Article the twelfth. The powers not delegated to the United States by the Constitution, nor prohibited by it to the States, are reserved to the States respectively, or to the people.

ATTEST,

Frederick Augustus Muhlenberg, Speaker of the House of Representatives.

John Adams, Vice President of the United States, and President of the Senate.

John Beckley, Clerk of the House of Representatives.

Sam. A. Otis, Secretary of the Senate.

Freedom of Religion, Speech, Press, Assembly

AMENDMENT I

Congress shall make no law **respecting** an establishment of **religion**, or **prohibiting** the free exercise thereof; or abridging the **freedom** of **speech**, or of the **press**; or the right of the people peaceably to **assemble**, and to **petition** the Government for a redress of grievances.

Right To Bear Arms

AMENDMENT II

A well regulated Militia, being **necessary** to the **security** of a free State, the right of the **people** to keep and **bear Arms**, shall not be infringed.

Quartering Soldiers

AMENDMENT III

No **Soldier** shall, in time of peace be **quartered** in any house, without the consent of the Owner, nor in time of war, but in a manner to be prescribed by law.

Unreasonable Searches and Seizures

AMENDMENT IV

The right of the people to be secure in their persons, houses, papers, and effects, against **unreasonable searches** and **seizures**, shall not be

EASY

violated, and no Warrants shall issue, but upon probable cause, supported by Oath or affirmation, and particularly describing the place to be searched, and the persons or things to be seized.

Self-Incrimination, Due Process of Law

AMENDMENT V

No person shall be held to answer for a **capital**, or otherwise infamous crime, unless on a presentment or indictment of a **Grand** Jury, except in cases arising in the **land** or **naval** forces, or in the Militia, when in actual service in time of War or public danger; nor shall any person be subject for the same offence to be twice put in jeopardy of life or limb; nor shall be compelled in any criminal case to be a witness against himself, nor be deprived of life, liberty, or property, without due process of law; nor shall private property be taken for public use, without just compensation.

EASY

RESPECTING	NECESSARY	SEARCHES
RELIGION	SECURITY	SEIZURES
PROHIBITING	PEOPLE	CAPITAL
FREEDOM	BEAR	GRAND
SPEECH	ARMS	LAND
PRESS	SOLDIER	NAVAL
ASSEMBLE	QUARTERED	
PETITION	UNREASONABLE	

– TRIVIA WORD SEARCH –
(TWO WORDS)

Eminent Domain Clause.

What must a person receive if private property is taken from them for public use?

_____

_____

EASY

```
U  S  E  R  U  Z  I  E  S  Y  P  A  U  C  S  Y  S
P  U  L  T  Q  C  A  N  N  Y  O  S  O  T  E  Z  I
B  G  B  U  H  W  J  R  R  G  D  E  X  K  H  A  O
T  M  A  N  O  I  T  A  S  N  E  P  M  O  C  G  T
R  Q  N  P  G  P  S  M  Q  I  R  D  E  E  R  G  P
A  Z  O  K  J  S  O  P  Z  T  E  B  J  O  A  R  D
E  T  S  P  E  D  P  E  T  I  T  I  O  N  E  A  M
B  R  A  C  E  B  P  X  Y  B  R  B  R  S  S  N  D
Y  U  E  E  A  L  A  Y  E  I  A  M  S  D  P  D  A
Q  N  R  S  G  P  P  A  R  H  U  Y  K  N  E  E  S
T  F  N  E  P  R  I  O  I  O  Q  U  A  A  E  D  S
R  O  U  C  L  E  T  T  E  R  C  Z  Q  L  C  H  E
Y  N  K  U  U  I  C  S  A  P  S  N  A  Y  H  H  M
G  X  P  R  V  D  G  T  U  L  Q  V  S  M  J  L  B
K  I  E  I  M  L  J  I  I  J  A  Y  I  K  U  E  L
L  F  N  T  U  O  I  Y  O  N  V  Q  J  P  N  Q  E
N  W  D  Y  O  S  M  R  A  N  G  T  P  T  E  L  Z
```

EASY

Right to Public Trial by Jury

AMENDMENT VI

In all criminal prosecutions, the accused shall enjoy the right to a speedy and public trial, by an impartial jury of the State and district wherein the crime shall have been committed, which district shall have been previously ascertained by law, and to be informed of the nature and cause of the accusation; to be confronted with the witnesses against him; to have compulsory process for obtaining witnesses in his favor, and to have the Assistance of Counsel for his defence.

Right To Trial by Jury for Federal Civil Cases

AMENDMENT VII

In Suits at common law, where the value in controversy shall exceed twenty dollars, the right of trial by jury shall be preserved, and no fact tried by a jury, shall be otherwise re-examined in any Court of the United States, than according to the rules of the common law.

Prohibits Cruel and Unusual Punishments

AMENDMENT VIII

Excessive bail shall not be required, nor excessive fines imposed, nor cruel and unusual punishments inflicted.

MEDIUM

Rights Not Listed Belong to The People

AMENDMENT IX

The enumeration in the Constitution, of certain rights, shall not be construed to deny or disparage others retained by the people.

Rights Not Listed Belong to The People

AMENDMENT X

The powers not delegated to the United States by the Constitution, nor prohibited by it to the States, are reserved to the States respectively, or to the people.

MEDIUM

Answer the following questions to reveal a word from the preceding exert. Next, find the word in the puzzle.

1. Which amendment guarantees the right to a speedy and public trial? (1 word)
   _____

2. According to the Sixth Amendment, in what type of court must the accused be tried? (5 words)
   _____

3. What right does the Sixth Amendment provide regarding witnesses against the accused? (1 word)
   _____

4. Under the Sixth Amendment, what right does the accused have regarding witnesses in their favor? (4 words)
   _____

5. Which amendment protects against excessive bail? (1 word)
   _____

6. What does the Eighth Amendment prohibit in terms of punishment? (2 words)
   _____

7. According to the Seventh Amendment, what is preserved in suits at common law where the value in controversy exceeds twenty dollars? (4 words)
   _____

8. According to the Tenth Amendment, who holds the powers not delegated to the United States by the Constitution, nor prohibited by it to the states? (2 words)
   _____

9. Which amendment ensures that rights not specifically mentioned in the Constitution are still protected? (1 word)
   _____

MEDIUM

```
H  X  L  X  D  Z  S  G  N  I  Q  A  E  S  E  U
Q  C  R  U  N  U  S  U  A  L  L  E  U  R  C  B
S  T  V  A  I  V  E  Q  V  I  D  M  Q  I  N  H
E  T  R  C  L  T  C  O  B  T  A  I  N  G  T  T
K  E  A  I  O  B  O  J  W  X  O  R  H  H  S  B
M  L  L  T  A  M  R  X  S  M  Q  C  G  T  B  G
Z  T  B  S  E  L  P  P  R  F  D  I  O  Y  B  D
H  V  K  F  Z  W  B  U  L  P  E  S  L  E  D  E
Q  I  O  L  C  K  H  Y  L  N  T  P  L  I  O  T
V  U  G  W  T  E  P  E  J  S  N  P  S  T  W  T
D  L  T  S  I  X  T  H  R  U  O  T  R  N  Z  I
O  J  R  W  E  R  O  D  N  E  R  R  P  D  K  M
U  O  D  A  S  T  X  I  P  I  F  Y  Y  K  V  M
F  Q  J  J  E  E  A  X  C  A  N  P  B  Y  C  O
P  Z  N  L  C  X  R  T  J  T  O  T  R  V  L  C
Q  K  F  S  W  N  F  N  S  K  C  O  H  F  N  I
```

AMENDMENTS 11-27

RATIFIED

Each date varies. An amendment becomes valid only when ratified by the legislatures of, or conventions in, three-fourths of the states (i.e., 38 of 50 states).

PURPOSE

The Amendments to the Constitution serve the crucial purpose of modifying or adding provisions to the original document to address evolving societal needs, protect individual rights, and refine the structure of the government. This demonstrates the Constitution's capacity to remain relevant and responsive over time, which reflects the intent of the original framers.

Third
Congress of the United States;
At the First session.

Begun and held at the City of
Philadelphia, in the State of Pennsylvania, on Monday the Second of
December one thousand seven hundred
and ninety three.

Resolved by the Senate and House of Representatives of the United States of America in Congress assembled,

Limits On Suing States

AMENDMENT XI

Passed by Congress March 4, 1794. Ratified February 7, 1795.

Note: Article III, section 2, of the Constitution was modified by amendment 11.

The Judicial power of the United States shall not be construed to extend to any suit in law or equity, commenced or prosecuted against one of the United **States** by Citizens of another State, or by Citizens or Subjects of any Foreign State.

Separate Electoral College Ballots for President & VP

AMENDMENT XII

Passed by Congress December 9, 1803. Ratified June 15, 1804.

Note: A portion of Article II, section 1 of the Constitution was superseded by the 12th amendment.

The Electors shall meet in their respective states and vote by ballot for President and Vice-President, one of whom, at least, shall not be an inhabitant of the same state with themselves; they shall name in their ballots the person voted for as President, and in distinct ballots the person voted for as Vice-President, and they shall make distinct lists of all persons voted for as President, and of all persons voted for as Vice-President, and of the number of votes for each, which lists they shall sign and certify, and transmit sealed to the seat of the government of the United States, directed to the President of the Senate; -- the President of the Senate shall, in the presence of the Senate and

MEDIUM

House of Representatives, open all the certificates and the votes shall then be counted; -- The person having the greatest number of votes for President, shall be the President, if such number be a majority of the whole number of Electors appointed; and if no person have such majority, then from the persons having the highest numbers not exceeding three on the list of those voted for as President, the House of **Representatives** shall choose immediately, by ballot, the President. But in choosing the President, the votes shall be taken by states, the representation from each state having one vote; a quorum for this purpose shall consist of a member or members from two-thirds of the states, and a majority of all the states shall be necessary to a choice. [And if the House of Representatives shall not choose a President whenever the right of choice shall devolve upon them, before the fourth day of March next following, then the Vice-President shall act as President, as in case of the death or other constitutional disability of the President. --]* The person having the greatest number of votes as Vice-President, shall be the Vice-President, if such number be a majority of the whole number of Electors appointed, and if no person have a majority, then from the two highest numbers on the list, the Senate shall choose the Vice-President; a quorum for the purpose shall consist of two-thirds of the whole number of Senators, and a majority of the whole number shall be necessary to a choice. But no person constitutionally ineligible to the office of President shall be eligible to that of Vice-President of the United States.

*Superseded by section 3 of the 20th amendment.

MEDIUM

1. Against which does the Eleventh Amendment prohibit federal courts from hearing cases? (1 word)

2. The Eleventh Amendment prevents the Judicial power of the U.S. from hearing cases involving states being sued by individuals not of that state. Which jurisdictions are responsible for exercising this power? (2 words)

3. Who chooses the President if no candidate receives a majority of electoral votes for President? (1 word)

4. When no candidate receives a majority of electoral votes for President, and the President must be chosen, from the top candidates how many are considered? (1 word)

5. Who chooses the Vice President if no candidate receives a majority of electoral votes for Vice President? (1 word)

6. When no candidate receives a majority of electoral votes for Vice President, and the VP must be chosen, from the top VP candidates how many are considered? (1 word)

7. Can an individual who is ineligible to be President be elected as Vice President according to the Twelfth Amendment? (1 word)

8. What eligibility requirements must an individual who is ineligible to be President have to be elected as Vice President? (1 word)

9. What was one major flaw in the original electoral process that the Twelfth Amendment aimed to fix? (1 word)

10. Two-thirds of Representatives and Senators must concur when respectively voting under the Twelfth Amendment. What does this number constitute? (1 word)

MEDIUM

```
Q F O U R T Q A O M K X S O F H B O Y W
V X L E Y T E E F R K B G T L S D U A W
L X B H X E H W Z Q I O C F R T F Q H Q
J V V V R T J K G A H O V O A U Z A Q S
Z T E M P A T L C A D R E W S H O Y S D
T N K J L T W O D U H F T I O Q V C B M
Y N G B P S T O Q S K F A O O V P Z L R
D X C N O C B N C N A F N D V I X G Z U
W S E A R U F S E S I A E Q V N F N X N
I Z G E B P B E I V O G S Z F I P I Z M
S K I U R K T N E D I S E R P E R M M U
Q T N F P H G R H M F Y V N M R E A P R
Y H A I G X T E N J E N E D B I Y L V O
C R R I N V X Z I X D P N L N F Z T H U
E C E K R E P R E S E N T A T I V E S Q
C U H Q L I T W E M R Z E B M B G N I M
I B T B D U A Y M O A E E L D V W Q H T
V T D R A W R H A W L B N R X O X N V J
I M Z L F N S E S L T L Z Z O B K A O O
T F M N H M Z Y Y L K M T K T H I H L I
```

MEDIUM

Abolishes Slavery

AMENDMENT XIII

Passed by Congress January 31, 1865. Ratified December 6, 1865.

Note: A portion of Article IV, section 2, of the Constitution was superseded by the 13th amendment.

Section 1.

Neither slavery nor involuntary servitude, except as a punishment for crime whereof the party shall have been duly convicted, shall exist within the United States, or any place subject to their jurisdiction.

Section 2.

Congress shall have power to enforce this article by appropriate legislation.

Citizenship, Due Process, Equal Protection

AMENDMENT XIV

Passed by Congress June 13, 1866. Ratified July 9, 1868.

Note: Article I, section 2, of the Constitution was modified by section 2 of the 14th amendment.

Section 1.

All persons **born** or naturalized in the United States, and subject to the jurisdiction thereof, are citizens of the United States and of the State wherein they reside. No State shall make or enforce any law which shall abridge the

MEDIUM

privileges or immunities of citizens of the United States; nor shall any State deprive any person of life, liberty, or property, without due process of law; nor deny to any person within its jurisdiction the equal protection of the laws.

Section 2.

Representatives shall be apportioned among the several States according to their respective numbers, counting the whole number of persons in each State, excluding Indians not taxed. But when the right to vote at any election for the choice of electors for President and Vice-President of the United States, Representatives in Congress, the Executive and Judicial officers of a State, or the members of the Legislature thereof, is denied to any of the **male** inhabitants of such State, being twenty-one years of age,* and citizens of the United States, or in any way abridged, except for participation in rebellion, or other crime, the basis of representation therein shall be reduced in the proportion which the number of such male citizens shall bear to the whole number of male citizens twenty-one years of age in such State.

Section 3.

No person shall be a Senator or Representative in Congress, or elector of President and Vice-President, or hold any office, civil or military, under the United States, or under any State, who, having previously taken an oath, as a member of Congress, or as an officer of the United States, or as a member of any State legislature, or as an executive or judicial officer of any State, to support the Constitution of the United States, shall have engaged in **insurrection** or rebellion against the same, or given aid or comfort to the enemies thereof. But Congress may by a vote of two-thirds of each House, remove such disability.

Section 4.

MEDIUM

The validity of the public debt of the United States, authorized by law, including debts incurred for payment of pensions and bounties for services in suppressing insurrection or rebellion, shall not be questioned. But neither the United States nor any State shall assume or pay any debt or obligation incurred in aid of insurrection or rebellion against the United States, or any claim for the loss or emancipation of any slave; but all such debts, obligations and claims shall be held illegal and void.

Section 5.

The Congress shall have the power to enforce, by appropriate legislation, the provisions of this article.

Changed by section 1 of the 26th amendment.

Answer the following questions to reveal a word from the preceding exert.
Next, find the word in the puzzle.

1. What does the Thirteenth Amendment abolish?
   (3 words)

   _____

2. What does Section 1 of the Fourteenth Amendment
   define?
   (1 word)

   _____

3. What are two criteria necessary to be considered citizens
   of the United States?
   (2 words)

   _____

4. Are people subject to the jurisdiction of the United States
   considered citizens?
   (1 word)

   _____

5. What does the Fourteenth Amendment prohibit states
   from denying any person?
   (3 words)

   _____

6. What happens to the representation of a state if it
   denies the right to vote to male citizens over the age of
   21?
   (1 word)

   _____

MEDIUM

7. What acts disqualify individuals from holding any Federal or State office?
(4 words)

8. How can the disqualification from holding office by an individual be removed?
(1 word)

9. What power does Section 5 of the Fourteenth Amendment grant to Congress?
(1 word)

10. In what year was the Fourteenth Amendment ratified?
(3 words)

11. For which citizens are states penalized in its apportionment of representation in Congress for denying the right to vote?
(1 word)

12. What is the status of debts incurred for insurrection or rebellion against the United States?
(2 words)

MEDIUM

```
S E R V I T U D E C S L J H K L B
L S Y N R N Z P B B D J Z Y V Z P
V M R R Y T S N I X H S W A L E R
T U A O E I X U O N A V O T E W O
A H T B X V L N R B R W U Y Y T
I Y N D P E A L E R L J T H G I E
P N U E A U C L E V E L T B F A C
R C L Z N P J R S G I C E C F I T
O W O I R J C I O W A G T B T D I
D D V L V F X Z C F N L N I E A O
G K N A A T M G S E N D Z M O R N
L K I R Y U U J E W Z E I K X N N
K C D U B A Q T S G N C S O Q B B
F G H T B L H E V S R U R J V L I
W E L A M G D N H O D S Y P Q B
R C C N I M G I J J N E X H V L E
L C S E Y P P G Y R Y R O N E O E
```

MEDIUM

Right to Vote (Men)

AMENDMENT XV

Passed by Congress February 26, 1869. Ratified February 3, 1870.

Section 1.

The right of citizens of the United States to vote shall not be denied or abridged by the United States or by any State on account of race, color, or previous condition of servitude--

Section 2.

The Congress shall have the power to enforce this article by appropriate legislation.

LEVY INCOME TAXES

AMENDMENT XVI

Passed by Congress July 2, 1909. Ratified February 3, 1913.

Note: Article I, section 9, of the Constitution was modified by amendment 16.

The Congress shall have power to lay and collect taxes on incomes, from whatever source derived, without apportionment among the several States, and without regard to any census or enumeration.

MEDIUM

Gives People the Right to Vote for Senators

AMENDMENT XVII

Passed by Congress May 13, 1912. Ratified April 8, 1913.

Note: Article I, section 3, of the Constitution was modified by the 17th amendment.

The Senate of the United States shall be composed of two Senators from each State, elected by the people thereof, for six years; and each Senator shall have one vote. The electors in each State shall have the qualifications requisite for electors of the most numerous branch of the State legislatures.

When vacancies happen in the representation of any State in the Senate, the executive authority of such State shall issue writs of election to fill such vacancies: Provided, That the legislature of any State may empower the executive thereof to make temporary appointments until the people fill the vacancies by election as the legislature may direct.

This amendment shall not be so construed as to affect the election or term of any Senator chosen before it becomes valid as part of the Constitution.

MEDIUM

Answer the following questions to reveal a word from the preceding exert. Next, find the word in the puzzle.

1. The Seventeenth Amendment was ratified in the year 19__?__.

2. What does the Fifteenth Amendment protect? (1 word)

3. Congress is allowed to levy a tax on __?__.

4. It is prohibited to deny the right to vote based on race, color, or previous condition of __?__.

5. Income taxes can be collected without apportionment among the __?__.

6. The Seventeenth Amendment established the direct election of __?__.

7. Prior to the Seventeenth Amendment, Senators were chosen by __?__.

8. Which amendment granted African American men the right to vote? (1 word)

9. How many Senators does each state have? (1 word)

10. How are vacancies in the Senate to be filled? (1 word)

11. Senators are elected to serve terms of how many years? (1 word)

12. What is the condition of appointments for Senatorial vacancies that are filled by the state on behalf of the people? (1 word)

MEDIUM

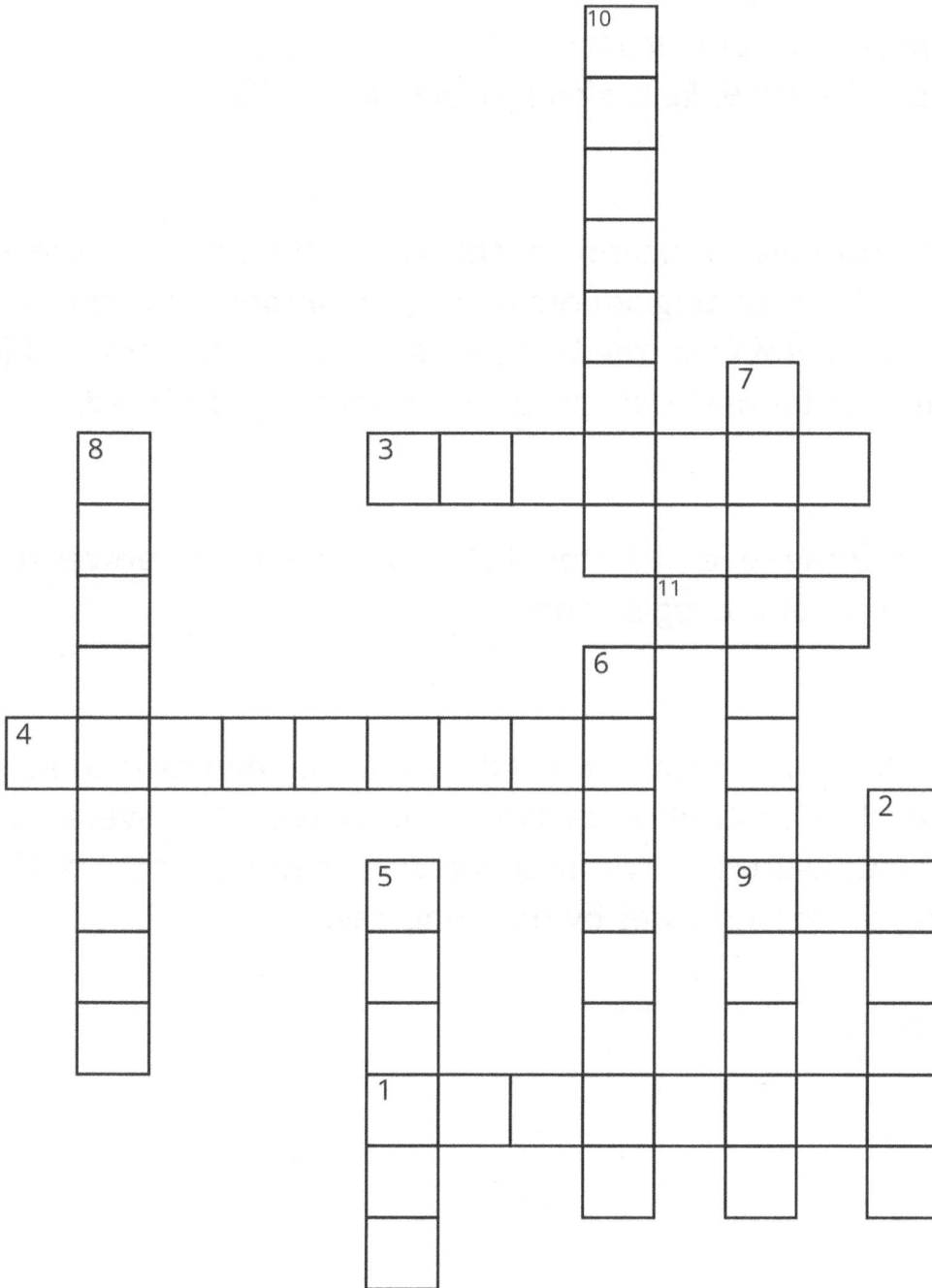

MEDIUM

Prohibition of Intoxicating Liquors

AMENDMENT XVIII

Passed by Congress December 18, 1917.
Ratified January 16, 1919. Repealed by amendment 21.

Section 1.

After one year from the ratification of this article the manufacture, sale, or transportation of intoxicating liquors within, the importation thereof into, or the exportation thereof from the United States and all territory subject to the jurisdiction thereof for beverage purposes is hereby prohibited.

Section 2.

The Congress and the several States shall have concurrent power to enforce this article by appropriate legislation.

Section 3.

This article shall be inoperative unless it shall have been ratified as an amendment to the Constitution by the legislatures of the several States, as provided in the Constitution, within seven years from the date of the submission hereof to the States by the Congress.

MEDIUM

Right to Vote (Women)

AMENDMENT XIX

*Passed by Congress June 4, 1919.
Ratified August 18, 1920.*

The right of citizens of the United States to vote shall not be denied or abridged by the United States or by any State on account of sex.

Congress shall have power to enforce this article by appropriate legislation.

1998 U.S. Stamp Commemorating the 19th Amendment.

ALSO HAPPENING IN THE YEAR 1919!

1. **Treaty of Versailles:** This treaty officially ended World War I. It imposed heavy reparations and territorial losses on Germany.
2. **League of Nations Established:** The precursor to the United Nations, was established to promote peace and prevent future conflicts.
3. **Prohibition:** The 18th Amendment established the prohibition of alcohol in the United States, leading to the Prohibition era in 1920.
4. **The Red Scare:** swept the U.S. driven by fears of communism, anarchism, and radicalism following the Russian Revolution.
5. **Race Riots:** The "Red Summer" of 1919 saw a wave of race riots.
6. **The Boston Police Strike:** sought better wages and working conditions. The strike was broken by the state militia, and the strikers were replaced, leading to a national debate on labor rights.
7. **The First Commercial Airline Flights:** The first regular international commercial flights began, marking the early days of modern aviation.

MEDIUM

Answer the following questions to reveal a word from the preceding exert.
Next, find the word in the puzzle.

1. The Eighteenth Amendment introduced the prohibition era in the United States. What prohibitions did it place on intoxicating liquors? (4 words)

_____

2. In addition to the United States, where else was this prohibition effective? (1 word)

_____

3. The Eighteenth Amendment was ratified in the year 19___? (1 word)

_____

4. The Eighteenth Amendment was repealed in the year 19___? (2 words)

_____

5. The enforcement of the Eighteenth Amendment was primarily the responsibility of which federal government body? (1 word)

_____

6. The Nineteenth Amendment sought to remedy the denial of the right to vote was based on ____ . (1 word)

_____

7. Which group of citizens was enfranchised by the Nineteenth Amendment? (1 word)

_____

8. What would become of the Eighteenth Amendment if it was not ratified after 7 years? (1 word)

_____

MEDIUM

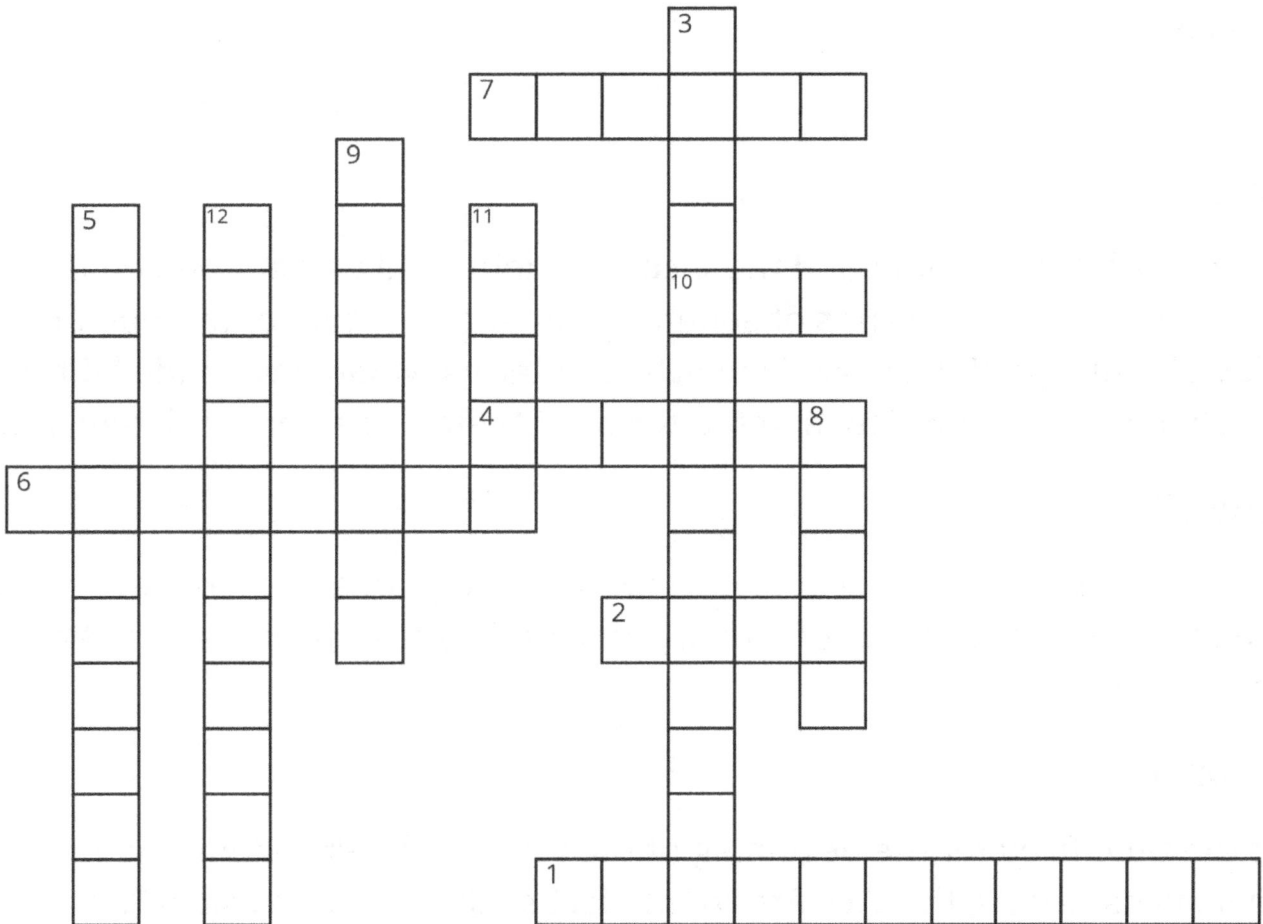

MEDIUM

Lame Duck Amendment

AMENDMENT XX

Passed by Congress March 2, 1932. Ratified January 23, 1933.

Note: Article I, section 4, of the Constitution was modified by section 2 of this amendment. In addition, a portion of the 12th amendment was superseded by section 3.

Section 1.

The terms of the President and the Vice President shall end at noon on the 20th day of January, and the terms of Senators and Representatives at noon on the 3d day of January, of the years in which such terms would have ended if this article had not been ratified; and the terms of their successors shall then begin.

Section 2.

The Congress shall assemble at least once in every year, and such meeting shall begin at noon on the 3d day of January, unless they shall by law appoint a different day.

Section 3.

If, at the time fixed for the beginning of the term of the President, the President elect shall have died, the Vice President elect shall become President. If a President shall not have been chosen before the time fixed for the beginning of his term, or if the President elect shall have failed to qualify, then the Vice President elect shall act as President until a President shall have qualified; and the Congress may by law provide for the case wherein neither a President elect nor a Vice President elect shall have qualified, declaring who shall then act as President, or the manner in which one who is to act shall be selected, and such

HARD

person shall act accordingly until a President or Vice President shall have qualified.

Section 4.

The Congress may by law provide for the case of the death of any of the persons from whom the House of Representatives may choose a President whenever the right of choice shall have devolved upon them, and for the case of the death of any of the persons from whom the Senate may choose a Vice President whenever the right of choice shall have devolved upon them.

Section 5.

Sections 1 and 2 shall take effect on the 15th day of October following the ratification of this article.

Section 6.

This article shall be inoperative unless it shall have been ratified as an amendment to the Constitution by the legislatures of three-fourths of the several States within seven years from the date of its submission.

HARD

Unscramble the following words to reveal a word from the preceding exert.
Next, find the word in the puzzle.

1.   LEDODVEV

2.   FADEILIQU

3.   BASELESM

4.   PVINERTAIEO

5.   TLEECSDE

6.   ESYRA

7.   ETRSM

8.   ARNYJUA

9.   GCDELRAIN

10.   ETIMGNE

11.   OHEICC

12.   ATIIOTAIFNRC

13.   SSECSOCURS

14.   RIODVEP

15.   TSETSA

16.   NRIEDPETS

17.   ALIDEF

18.   ROGSENSC

19.   BCTOROE

20.   ATEDH

HARD

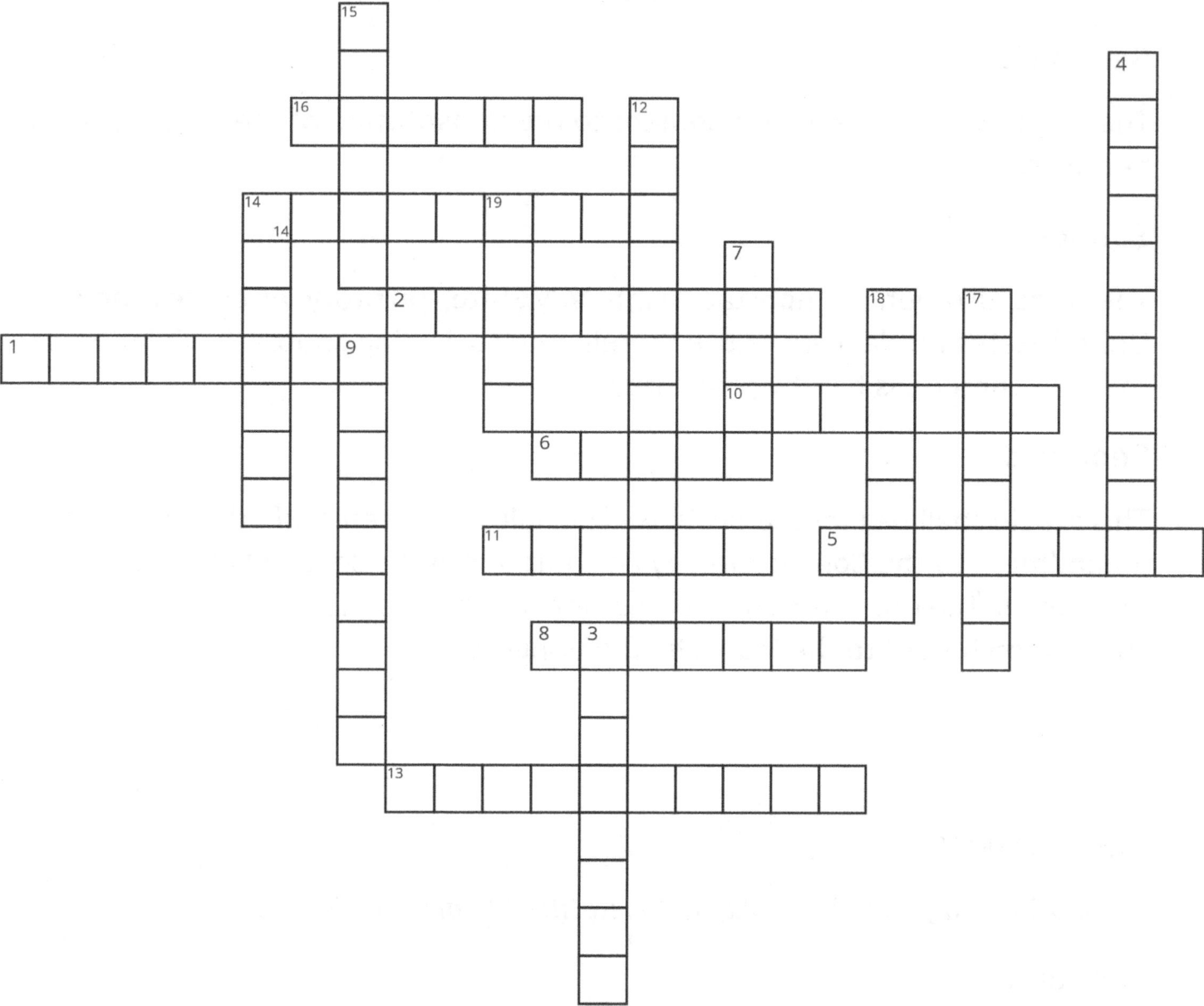

HARD

Repeals Prohibition

AMENDMENT XXI

Passed by Congress February 20, 1933. Ratified December 5, 1933.

Section 1.

The eighteenth article of amendment to the Constitution of the United States is hereby repealed.

Section 2.

The transportation or importation into any State, Territory, or possession of the United States for delivery or use therein of intoxicating liquors, in violation of the laws thereof, is hereby prohibited.

Section 3.

This article shall be inoperative unless it shall have been ratified as an amendment to the Constitution by conventions in the several States, as provided in the Constitution, within seven years from the date of the submission hereof to the States by the Congress.

Term Limits

AMENDMENT XXII

Passed by Congress March 21, 1947. Ratified February 27, 1951.

Section 1.

No person shall be elected to the office of the President more than twice, and no person who has held the office of President, or acted as President, for more than two years of a term to which some other person was elected President shall be elected to the office of the President more than once. But this Article

HARD

shall not apply to any person holding the office of President when this Article was proposed by the Congress, and shall not prevent any person who may be holding the office of President, or acting as President, during the term within which this Article becomes operative from holding the office of President or acting as President during the remainder of such term.

Section 2.

This article shall be inoperative unless it shall have been ratified as an amendment to the Constitution by the legislatures of three-fourths of the several States within seven years from the date of its submission to the States by the Congress.

HARD

Unscramble the following words to reveal a word from the preceding exert.
Next, find the word in the puzzle.

1.   **TSNOENCIVNO**

2.   **DOGHINL**

3.   **IRQSOLU**

4.   **HOSRTFU**

5.   **TMAPROTINOI**

6.   **ERRNIEDMA**

7.   **DSREIEPTN**

8.   **YRERTIROT**

9.   **TASTES**

10.   **DRELEAPE**

11.   **SNUMISOSIB**

12.   **EFCIOF**

13.   **NTILOAIVO**

14.   **SOPSENOSIS**

15.   **EERSALV**

16.   **VOEARTIPE**

17.   **MERT**

18.   **RIPTONSTNOTARA**

19.   **GCNITA**

20.   **PROHIBITED**

HARD

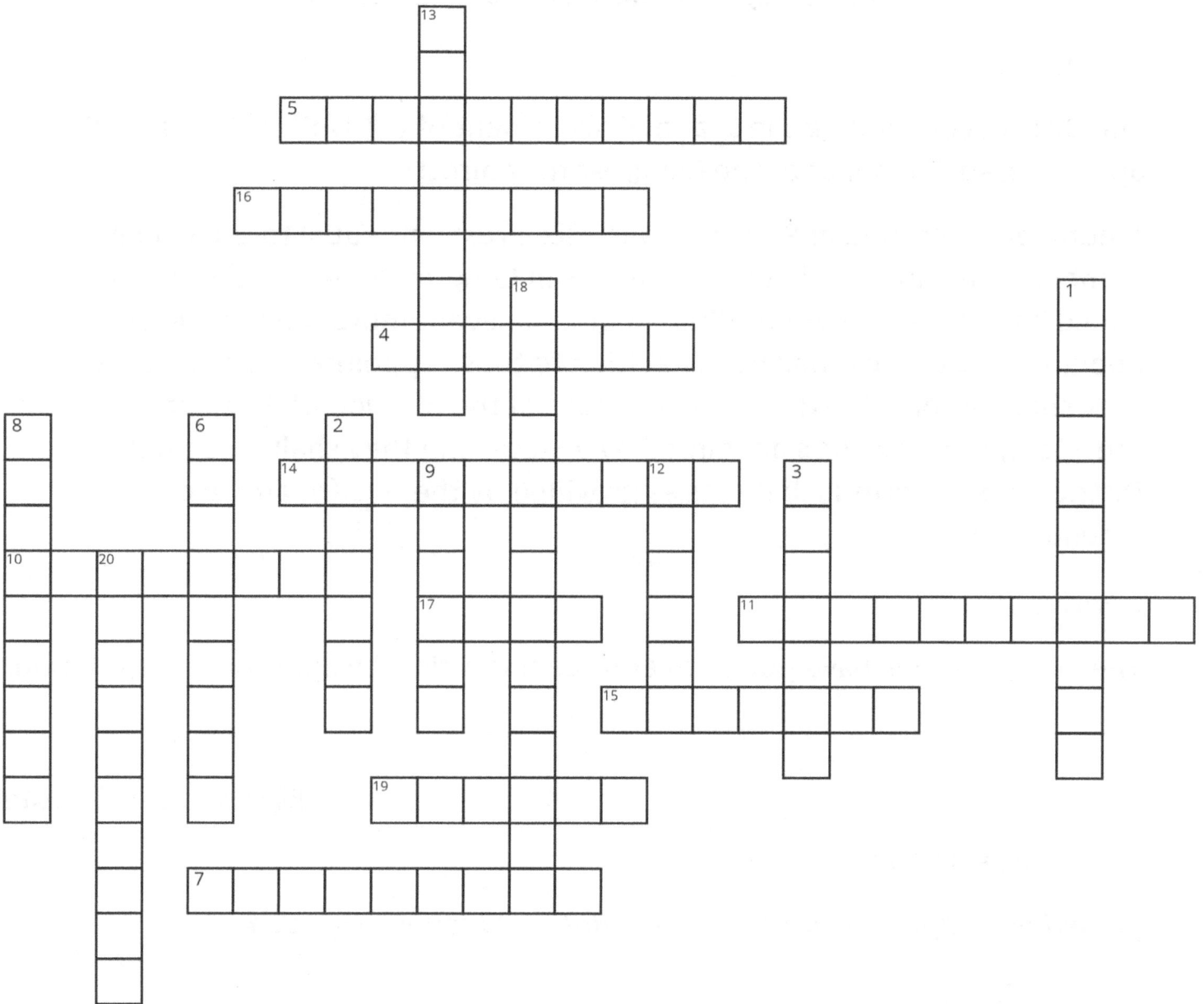

HARD

Presidential Voting Rights for Washington DC Citizens

AMENDMENT XXIII

Passed by Congress June 16, 1960. Ratified March 29, 1961.

Section 1.

The District constituting the seat of Government of the United States shall appoint in such manner as the Congress may direct:

A number of electors of President and Vice President equal to the whole number of Senators and Representatives in Congress to which the District would be entitled if it were a State, but in no event more than the least populous State; they shall be in addition to those appointed by the States, but they shall be considered, for the purposes of the election of President and Vice President, to be electors appointed by a State; and they shall meet in the District and perform such duties as provided by the twelfth article of amendment.

Section 2.

The Congress shall have power to enforce this article by appropriate legislation.

Eliminates Poll Taxes

AMENDMENT XXIV

Passed by Congress August 27, 1962. Ratified January 23, 1964.

Section 1.

The right of citizens of the United States to vote in any primary or other election for President or Vice President, for electors for President or Vice President, or for Senator or Representative in Congress, shall not be denied or

HARD

abridged by the United States or any State by reason of failure to pay any poll tax or other tax.

Section 2.

The Congress shall have power to enforce this article by appropriate legislation.

Unscramble the following words to reveal a word from the preceding exert.
Next, find the word in the puzzle.

1. **TECNISIZ**

2. **SCIDERDEON**

3. **UDIETS**

4. **EDIETTNL**

5. **RIFELUA**

6. **NEROCEF**

7. **NDEDEI**

8. **ICRTITDS**

9. **AIPNETDOP**

10. **WELTTHF**

11. **SEROPSUP**

12. **ENDUIT**

13. **GIRTH**

14. **SLOUPUOP**

15. **DRAGIBED**

16. **TELECOIN**

17. **FROMPRE**

18. **MEANNR**

19. **IDIOTDAN**

20. **WROPE**

HARD

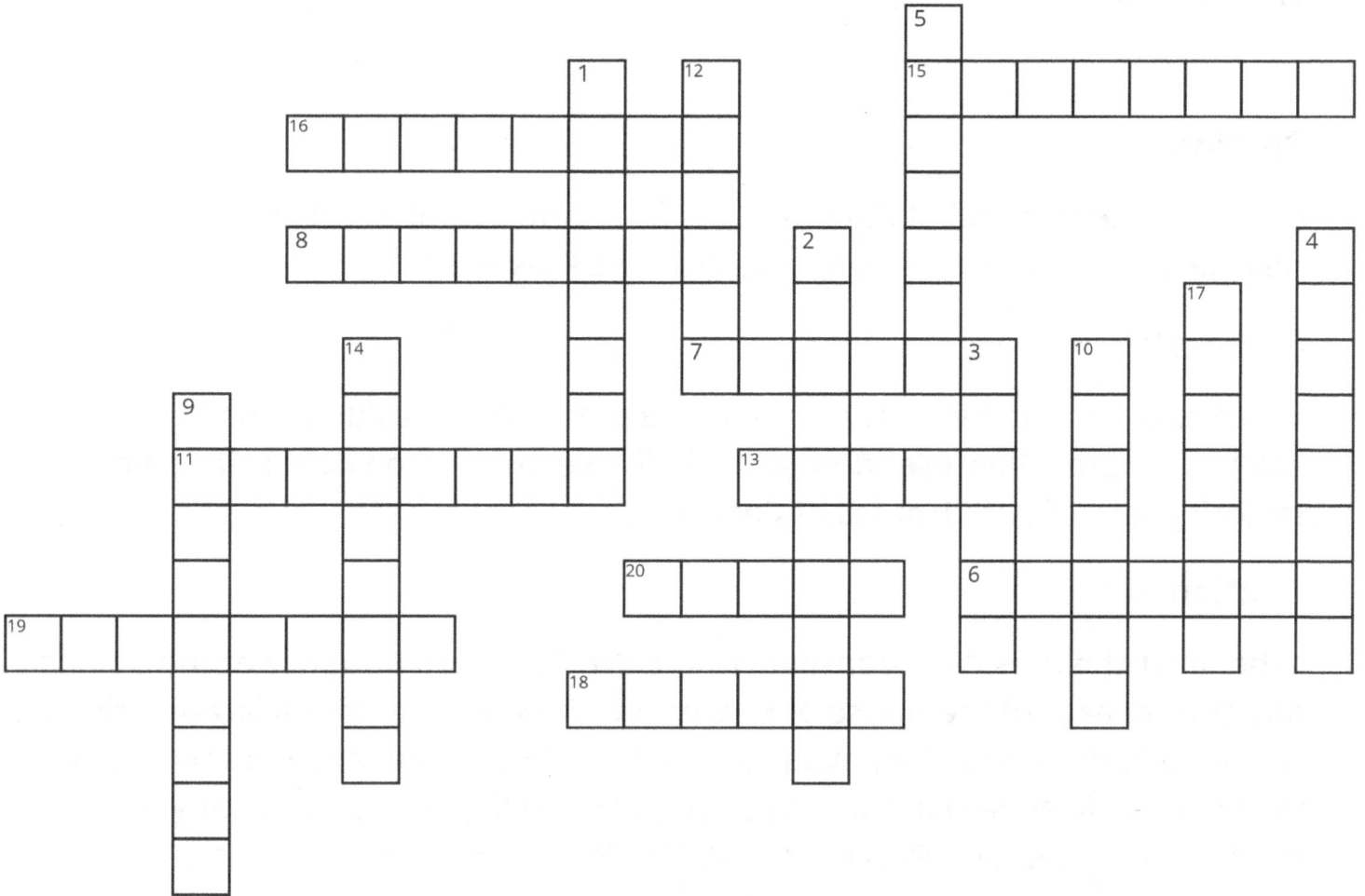

HARD

VP Succession

AMENDMENT XXV

Passed by Congress July 6, 1965. Ratified February 10, 1967.

Note: Article II, section 1, of the Constitution was affected by the 25th amendment.

Section 1.

In case of the removal of the President from office or of his death or resignation, the Vice President shall become President.

Section 2.

Whenever there is a vacancy in the office of the Vice President, the President shall nominate a Vice President who shall take office upon confirmation by a majority vote of both Houses of Congress.

Section 3.

Whenever the President transmits to the President pro tempore of the Senate and the Speaker of the House of Representatives his written declaration that he is unable to discharge the powers and duties of his office, and until he transmits to them a written declaration to the contrary, such powers and duties shall be discharged by the Vice President as Acting President.

Section 4.

Whenever the Vice President and a majority of either the principal officers of the executive departments or of such other body as Congress may by law provide, transmit to the President pro tempore of the Senate and the Speaker of the House of Representatives their written declaration that the President is

HARD

unable to discharge the powers and duties of his office, the Vice President shall immediately assume the powers and duties of the office as Acting President.

Thereafter, when the President transmits to the President pro tempore of the Senate and the Speaker of the House of Representatives his written declaration that no inability exists, he shall resume the powers and duties of his office unless the Vice President and a majority of either the principal officers of the executive department or of such other body as Congress may by law provide, transmit within four days to the President pro tempore of the Senate and the Speaker of the House of Representatives their written declaration that the President is unable to discharge the powers and duties of his office. Thereupon Congress shall decide the issue, assembling within forty-eight hours for that purpose if not in session. If the Congress, within twenty-one days after receipt of the latter written declaration, or, if Congress is not in session, within twenty-one days after Congress is required to assemble, determines by two-thirds vote of both Houses that the President is unable to discharge the powers and duties of his office, the Vice President shall continue to discharge the same as Acting President; otherwise, the President shall resume the powers and duties of his office.

HARD

Unscramble the following words to reveal a word from the preceding exert.
Next, find the word in the puzzle.

1.	**RIPCILANP**
2.	**YJMAOITR**
3.	**CAYCANV**
4.	**BLAENU**
5.	**MUSEER**
6.	**ESTANE**
7.	**MUSEAS**
8.	**TRENIONAIGS**
9.	**GISCHEDDAR**
10.	**MATEINON**
11.	**MYDIMETAILE**
12.	**TTPMEANDERS**
13.	**MALOVER**
14.	**CRATORYN**
15.	**SWEETHIRO**
16.	**TTWINER**
17.	**TGAINC**
18.	**KEEPARS**
19.	**RAMIFCOINNOT**
20.	**CARDIOLATEN**

HARD

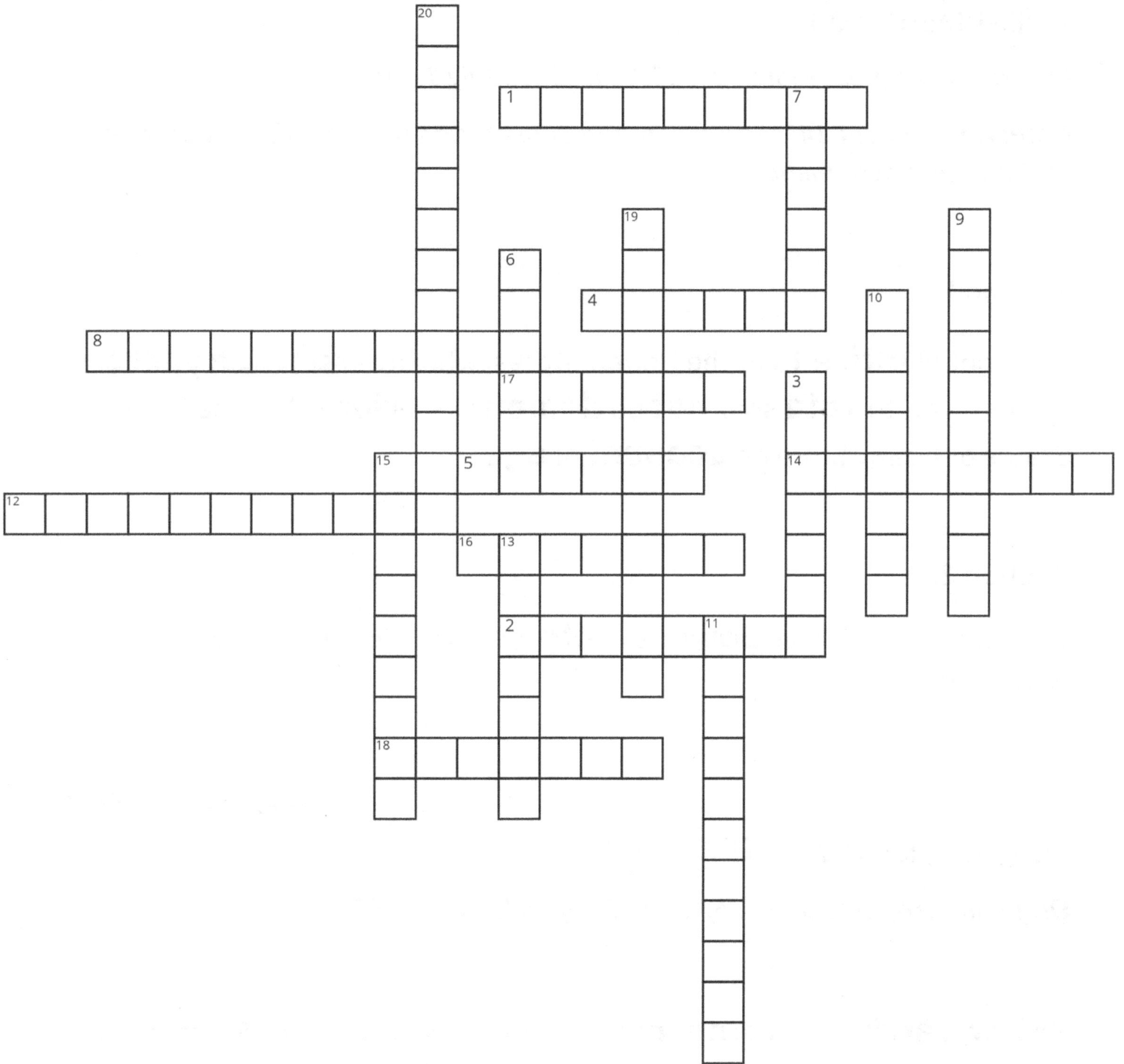

HARD

Legal Voting Age

AMENDMENT XXVI

Passed by Congress March 23, 1971. Ratified July 1, 1971.

Note: Amendment 14, section 2, of the Constitution was modified by section 1 of the 26th amendment.

Section 1.

The right of **citizens** of the United States, who are **eighteen years** of age or older, to **vote** shall **not** be **denied** or **abridged** by the United States or by any State on **account** of **age**.

Section 2.

The Congress shall have **power** to **enforce** this article by appropriate legislation.

Congress Pay Raises

AMENDMENT XXVII

Originally proposed Sept. 25, 1789. Ratified May 7, 1992.

No **law**, **varying** the **compensation** for the services of the Senators and Representatives, shall take **effect**, until an **election** of Representatives **shall** have **intervened**.

EASY

```
U  Z  E  C  R  O  F  N  E  S  X  J  A  R  H  L  A
C  Z  I  H  E  C  S  G  R  C  T  M  P  O  P  Q  G
C  P  K  T  O  G  H  C  Y  B  A  W  V  W  H  W  I
T  P  W  C  S  R  A  E  Y  W  P  G  O  W  Q  A  B
I  F  N  E  B  T  L  I  U  Q  N  R  B  C  B  D  A
M  N  O  F  L  Z  L  G  X  Q  M  U  I  U  M  C  S
E  F  T  F  K  C  O  H  F  S  H  T  V  I  C  Q  W
F  X  E  E  O  K  R  T  F  V  I  G  Y  O  M  B  P
D  Z  L  Y  R  M  K  E  W  Z  A  T  U  N  T  Z  A
H  U  E  Q  D  V  S  E  E  Q  W  N  O  M  V  E  M
R  D  C  O  M  P  E  N  S  A  T  I  O  N  A  N  W
F  U  T  Z  Z  L  S  N  G  I  Y  X  Y  O  R  T  F
A  P  I  L  H  A  C  C  E  I  V  Z  D  G  Y  C  X
C  A  O  A  H  B  D  E  G  D  I  R  B  A  I  C  V
M  B  N  W  T  Y  G  G  I  W  Y  D  E  I  N  E  D
L  D  L  S  E  N  O  C  L  E  A  I  A  J  G  D  Y
A  N  K  Q  O  R  Q  O  D  D  R  J  B  Z  I  S  C
```

EASY

THE PLEDGE OF ALLEGIANCE

is a patriotic verse that is recited to promise allegiance to the flag and republic of the United States of America. Originally authored in 1892 by socialist minister Francis Bellamy, it underwent 2 additional modifications. The final modification was made by President Eisenhower in 1954 and is the version recited today.

I pledge allegiance

to the Flag

of the United States of America,

and to the Republic

for which it stands,

one Nation under God,

indivisible, with liberty

and justice for all.

- TRIVIA WORD SEARCH -

When reciting the Pledge of Allegiance, a person should place their right _____ over their _____ while _____ the flag.

EASY

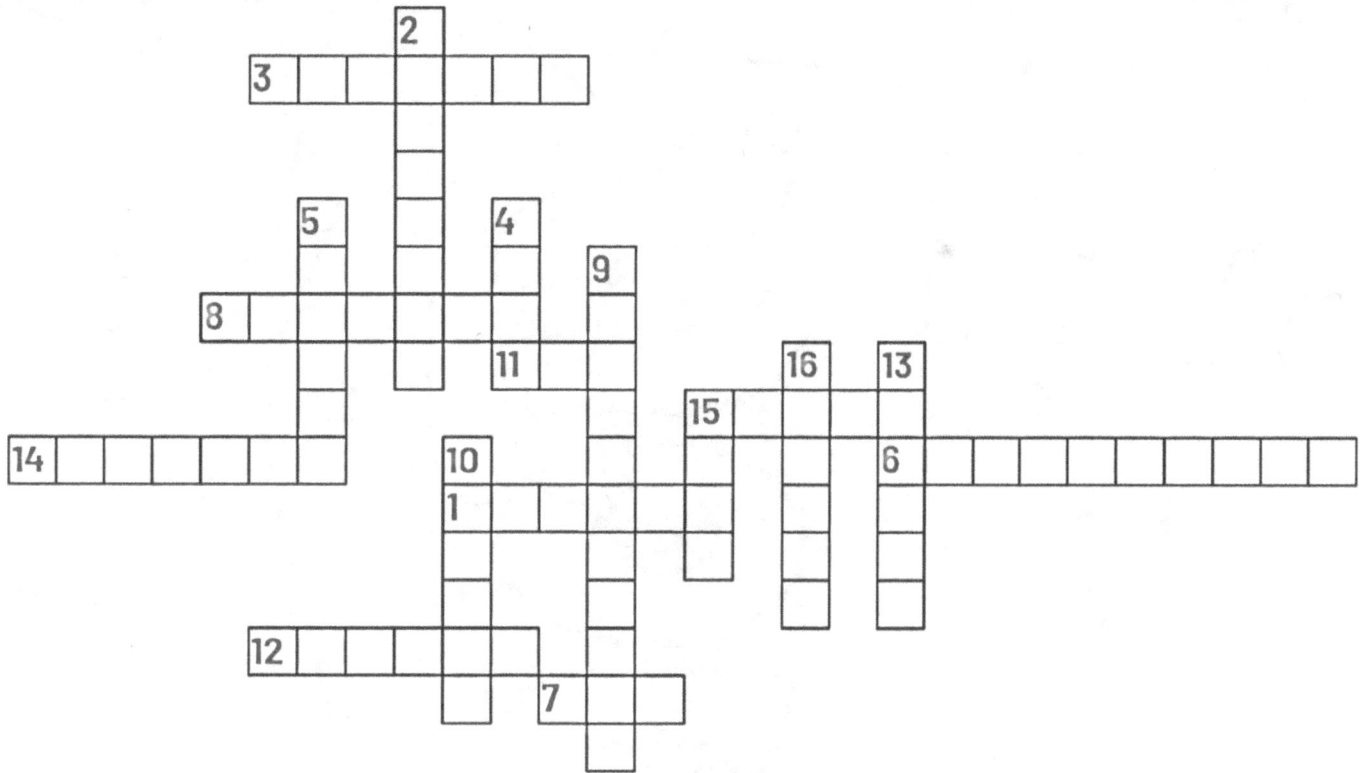

ACROSS

1. A body of united people.
3. Freedom without control, interference, or restrictions by authority.
6. Loyalty to a group.
7. The whole.
8. Named after amerigo vespucci.
11. Supreme being.
12. A community organized under one government.
14. Fair treatment according to proper law and principles.
15. Circulatory organ.

DOWN

2. A country where power is held by the people.
4. An emblem of a country.
5. A promise.
9. Cannot be separated.
10. Together to form a whole.
13. Represents.
15. The part of the arm beyond the wrist.
16. Positioned in a certain direction of.

EASY

THE CONSTITUTION

PUZZLE ONE:
The <u>ARTICLES</u> of <u>CONFEDERATION</u>.

PUZZLE TWO:
The <u>SENATE</u> and the House of <u>REPRESENTATIVES</u>.

PUZZLE THREE:
Every two years, <u>ONE-THIRD</u> of the Senate's members are elected (or reelected).

PUZZLE FOUR:
<u>YEAS</u> and <u>NAYS</u>.

PUZZLE FIVE:
If the President rejects a bill, it can still become law if both the House and Senate override the <u>VETO</u> with a two-thirds majority vote in each chamber.

PUZZLE SIX:
No Appropriation of Money to "raise and support" an army shall be for a longer Term than <u>TWO YEARS</u>.

PUZZLE SEVEN:
No <u>TITLE</u> of <u>NOBILITY</u> shall be granted by the United States.

PUZZLE EIGHT:

1. EXECUTIVE

2. ELECTORS

3. SENATORS, REPRESENTATIVES, or PERSONS holding an Office of Trust or Profit under the United States.

4. The day shall be the SAME throughout the United States as determined by Congress.

5. NATURAL BORN CITIZEN, at least attained to the AGE of THIRTY-FIVE YEARS, and a RESIDENT within the United States for 14 years.

6. The VICE PRESIDENT.

7. A Compensation, which shall neither be ENCREASED nor DIMINISHED during the Period for which he shall have been elected,

8. An OATH or AFFIRMATION.

9. CONGRESS

10. The House of Representatives must CHUSE the President from the candidates who tied.

11. I do solemnly swear (or affirm) that I will faithfully execute the Office of President of the United States, and will to the best of my Ability, preserve, protect and defend the CONSTITUTION of the United States.

PUZZLE NINE:

1. The MILITIA of the several States

2. REPRIEVES and PARDONS

3. The SENATE

4. TWO-THIRDS

5. AMBASSADORS, other public MINISTERS and CONSULS, JUDGES of the Supreme Court, and all other OFFICERS of the United States

6. The President can fill up all Vacancies by GRANTING COMMISSIONS WHICH SHALL EXPIRE at the end of the Senate's next session.

7. Information on the STATE of the UNION

8. EXTRAORDINARY

9. That the Laws be FAITHFULLY EXECUTED

10. COMMISSION all the Officers of the United States

11. IMPEACHMENT and CONVICTION

PUZZLE TEN:

1. JUDICIAL
2. During **GOOD BEHAVIOR** (for life, unless they are impeached and removed)
3. Their **COMPENSATION** (salary)
4. Cases arising under the **CONSTITUTION**, the **LAWS** of the United States, and **TREATIES** made.
5. Article **THREE**, Section **TWO**
6. **APPELLATE JURISDICTION**
7. They shall be by **JURY**
8. In the **STATE** where the said crimes shall have been **COMMITTED**
9. **ADHERING** to enemies and **GIVING** them **AID** and **COMFORT**
10. The testimony of two **WITNESSES** to the same overt act, or a **CONFESSION** in open court
11. **CONGRESS**
12. No attainder of treason shall work corruption of blood, or forfeiture except during the **LIFE** of the person attainted.
13. **CHECKS** and **BALANCES**

PUZZLE ELEVEN:

1. TERRITORY
2. FELONY
3. PRIVILEGES
4. RULES
5. JURISDICTION
6. PROPERTY
7. FAITH
8. CONSENT
9. PREJUDICE
10. JUSTICE
11. GUARANTEE
12. TREASON
13. REGULATIONS
14. ESCAPING
15. ADMITTED
16. RECORDS
17. REPUBLICAN
18. IMMUNITIES
19. JUNCTION
20. CRIME

PUZZLE TWELVE:

1. WHENEVER
2. SUFFRAGE
3. VALID
4. AMENDMENTS
5. CONVENTION
6. THOUSAND
7. HOUSES
8. SENATE
9. DEPRIVED
10. LEGISLATURES
11. NECESSARY
12. MANNER
13. STATES
14. PROPOSE
15. RATIFICATION
16. INTENTS
17. PURPOSES
18. APPLICATION
19. CLAUSES
20. SEVERAL

PUZZLE THIRTEEN:

1. PURSUANCE
2. OFFICERS
3. AUTHORITY
4. VALID
5. RELIGIOUS
6. BOUND
7. MEMBERS
8. DEBTS
9. AFFIRMATION
10. TREATIES
11. AGAINST
12. EXECUTIVE
13. ADOPTION
14. TRUST
15. SUPREME
16. CONTRARY
17. ENGAGEMENTS
18. REQUIRED
19. CONFEDERATION
20. MENTIONED

PUZZLE FOURTEEN:

1. WASHINGTON
2. UNANIMOUS
3. WILLIAMSON
4. BETWEEN
5. HAMILTON
6. INTERLINED
7. PRESENT
8. DICKINSON
9. SUFFICIENT
10. WITNESS
11. LIVINGSTON
12. CONSENT
13. RATIFYING
14. SEPTEMBER
15. MADISON
16. ATTEST
17. WILSON
18. FRANKLIN
19. CONVENTIONS
20. SECRETARY

THE BILL OF RIGHTS

PUZZLE FIFTEEN:

nor shall private property be taken for public use, without <u>JUST COMPENSATION</u>.

PUZZLE SIXTEEN:

1. The **SIXTH** Amendment.

2. A court in the **STATE** and **DISTRICT WHERE** the **CRIME** was **COMMITTED**.

3. The right to be **CONFRONTED** with the witnesses against them.

4. The right to **OBTAIN** witnesses in their favor through **COMPULSORY PROCESS**.

5. The **EIGHTH** Amendment.

6. **CRUEL** and **UNUSUAL** punishment.

7. The **RIGHT** of **TRIAL BY JURY**.

8. The **STATES** or the **PEOPLE**.

9. The **NINTH** Amendment.

AMENDMENTS 11-27

PUZZLE SEVENTEEN:

1. Cases in which a **STATE** is sued by citizens of another state or a foreign country.

2. To limit the jurisdiction of **FEDERAL COURTS** in cases involving states.

3. **SEVENTEEN NINETY-FIVE**

4. The House of **REPRESENTATIVES**.

5. The House of Representatives chooses the President from the top **THREE** candidates.

6. The **SENATE**.

7. The Senate chooses the Vice President from the top **TWO** candidates.

8. **NO**

9. They must meet the **SAME** eligibility requirements as a President.

10. The **VICE PRESIDENT** who is the President of the Senate.

11. The **TIE** in electoral votes between presidential and vice-presidential candidates from the same party.

12. **EIGHTEEN ZERO FOUR**

13. **QUORUM**

PUZZLE EIGHTEEN:

1. **SLAVERY** and **INVOLUNTARY SERVITUDE**, except as punishment for a crime.

2. Defines **CITIZENSHIP** and provides equal protection under the law.

3. All persons **BORN** or **NATURALIZED** in the United States, and subject to its jurisdiction.

4. **YES**

5. **EQUAL PROTECTION** of the **LAWS**.

6. The state's representation in Congress is **REDUCED**.

7. Those who have engaged in **INSURRECTION** or **REBELLION** against the United States or **GIVEN AID** to its enemies, after having taken an oath to support the Constitution.

8. By a two-thirds **VOTE** of each house of Congress.

9. The power to **ENFORCE** the provisions of the amendment by appropriate legislation.

10. **EIGHTEEN SIXTY EIGHT**

11. **MALE** citizens over the age of 21.

12. Such debts are **ILLEGAL** and **VOID**.

PUZZLE NINETEEN:

1. THIRTEEN
2. VOTING
3. INCOMES
4. SERVITUDE
5. STATES
6. SENATORS
7. LEGISLATURES
8. FIFTEENTH
9. TWO
10. ELECTION
11. SIX
12. TEMPORARY

PUZZLE TWENTY:

1. MANUFACTURE
2. SALE
3. TRANSPORTATION
4. EXPORT
5. TERRITORIES
6. NINETEEN
7. THIRTY
8. THREE
9. CONGRESS
10. SEX
11. WOMEN
12. INOPERATIVE

PUZZLE TWENTY-ONE:

1. DEVOLVED
2. QUALIFIED
3. ASSEMBLE
4. INOPERATIVE
5. SELECTED
6. YEARS
7. TERMS
8. JANUARY
9. DECLARING
10. MEETING
11. CHOICE
12. RATIFICATION
13. SUCCESSORS
14. PROVIDE
15. STATES
16. PRESIDENT
17. FAILED
18. CONGRESS
19. OCTOBER
20. DEATH

PUZZLE TWENTY-TWO:

1. CONVENTIONS
2. HOLDING
3. LIQUORS
4. FOURTHS
5. IMPORTATION
6. REMAINDER
7. PRESIDENT
8. TERRITORY
9. STATES
10. REPEALED
11. SUBMISSION
12. OFFICE
13. VIOLATION
14. POSSESSION
15. SEVERAL
16. OPERATIVE
17. TERM
18. TRANSPORTATION
19. ACTING
20. PROHIBITED

PUZZLE TWENTY-THREE:

1. CITIZENS
2. CONSIDERED
3. DUTIES
4. ENTITLED
5. FAILURE
6. ENFORCE
7. DENIED
8. DISTRICT
9. APPOINTED
10. TWELFTH
11. PURPOSES
12. UNITED
13. RIGHT
14. POPULOUS
15. ABRIDGED
16. ELECTION
17. PERFORM
18. MANNER
19. ADDITION
20. POWER

PUZZLE TWENTY-FOUR:

1. PRINCIPAL
2. MAJORITY
3. VACANCY
4. UNABLE
5. RESUME
6. SENATE
7. ASSUME
8. RESIGNATION
9. DISCHARGED
10. NOMINATE
11. IMMEDIATELY
12. DEPARTMENTS
13. REMOVAL
14. CONTRARY
15. OTHERWISE
16. WRITTEN
17. ACTING
18. SPEAKER
19. CONFIRMATION
20. DECLARATION

PUZZLE 01

```
N C O B X U T L Z W J I T Q V Z J E
Y Q S U T U Y J T M G S S B K B L I
Y N N W V V E U M M H M O C G L R F
B F O Q A C I S H K S A H R D D O A
W R R I S I Y T R E B I L K D A H P
S P O S T E R I T Y M C V E R A S T
A W Y C Y A C C R Q J L S T P U I B
E S T G N S R E J W V M I P W J L N
T C I Z O A W E D M Y C H W G E B R
M B L G F R D I D O L U E N S P A Z
N O I N U D X L B E P L I S B B T C
M G U W S V Z D S H F P I Y R J S Y
O O Q O J Q D L K A H N N F F K E Y
D K N Z U T T R R H G I O R L H P R
S L A B I S E E Q S U R K C K N I H
C W R N T K K G T S M H Y P D W T X
C L T S Q M L R P H Q D B R P N Z D
D Y V K L L S L C K J A X K D X Q O
```

PUZZLE 02

```
B H C M U T N E M H C A E P M I O J Z Y
Z Q N A Y W D T Y F I V K S J W Z A O F
C E U I N R I A H Z H X C A U A A O G I
F P T V D I C T U Q Y D E S O P M O C L
V P V A E T R S B X F C V X P P R S M L
G R J I N S L E C J S L Y O U W Y Z Q Z
V T E S T E T V M E V M R B W N B O V S
H L M P A V S E C S E T S I L R V C V X
S I F S R Z Z N D M I P F Y E A R S V N
E R T V K E X M B O P V C L C S R D T F
I R E P R E S E N T A T I V E S O X T R
C S E W P H R E I G Y M T W S F O J U R
N S U V O S D N N D Y M I S R Y P N K W
A E E U M P W I Q T G M Z U O F T V E B
C R M X D G G N O M A Z E R T F M P J O
A G X W A X A B M C D T N P C K S O B R
V N P A H T I Z T A Z E I R E B M A L F
C O M T O U C S K M G P R V L N U Q W H
I C G U Q E F X A A P E P N E S O H C K
O D M G O K O L G O Q I N O I N U J R Q
```

PUZZLE 03

```
M R D S V P V J R A U I R F T Q
E F V Q P P R Z S O W Y Y M O L
D B Q T K P R O E C G R M N S T
C N M W N R D Z S D W S E G A X
S A E R E E D I S E R P T J J T
H R N V D S M K A L V E H G U T
L L O I U I W H L V K Q I Y S S
Q T V T R D W M C W T G R C T G
E I J H A E J V M A D N D E I B
D U B C O N V I C T E D M L C G
H Y G O I T E Y W Q I P J B E F
T R K B V L B S T I O W M A E W
I W L C H I E F X R H Z A I A B
P B O Q H C C H E D I G H L C W
Y W H P X E R E N I N H S I H M
I X S C T J J U N E Z I T I C B
```

PUZZLE 04

```
C T N E D E G D E L I V I R P T C
M A M F Z O R P S Y A N Q X E O S
B Y L I G K S U E J N O C S T J Y
I K E N I M R E T E D I J L R L G
M U R O U Q Q D Y A K T P K K E X
O J I O E G Y T Z H L A V D X Z C
E B A S P V I E Q A S S E M B L E
Y V U G M R S T A T E N I R M D S
R O M M O S E L U R L E S G N A J
H K L J R J I S N D E P C W E S A
Z O A R F U E A C H C M O Y T L T
H M N R W D R S X R T O N P D V N
U N R C R G O B H X I C G H E C Z
A A U B E E J L G T O B R F K Y A
A X O Q V X S F L C N Q E F U O Z
L E J V T C I T Q F S K S D J W O
W I L C Q K U P U B L I S H F R H
```

129

K L R R I D E S S A P E R Z I
B B K D S S L A N R U O J V O
H O U S E G W H P R V B K I N
O W E L M J N E T P T E G H X
T T U A A S N I V H R F T M B
E R N W N T O S D O I O G O E
V F E E E W B C U R Z R V B D
T X V R R C J M J I O E D E E
P R E S I D E N T G O C G S K
L D R B U R C P S I S E C N P
R E S O L U T I O N I U Z A H
C V P S L L I B U A U W C O R
P E V Y G V O T E T L D U K I
L R E T U R N Y Q E D S G D T
K Y R E D I S N O C E R M G M

PUZZLE 05

O D X B G E J E C R E M M O C W S D
S S E B K T H Z F A E S O Z T Q Q S
H M U M N A T G Y Z U N V N S E Y G
N V C E K L I S J Q V O X C E S S Z
P P I N S U R R E C T I O N S Y A E
M X N W R G S C O N S T I T U T E T
S W I S S E R P P U S A E G A C N O
F O V A D R Q Z X T G L S T B E D M
O A B T R I B U N A L S H A M L S O
N R O I G B S M R W C I D N O L S R
T E R K J H Y E A R S G R W P O W P
N O R R Z K O O S C S E W M Z C O H
E W O A E Y K N I T V L C T H S S Y
J T W W L E F E A O R N K I T H O Z
I A S E N C N X G S P A Y L F Q Z S
S W P Y L C E P H W Y Q H J Y F E X
X L L U E S G D B A B S S U G C O V
F J N Z H L M U L Z H T P E B G V P

PUZZLE 06

I R G I E M D M S Y L P S C U P
R T V Y S T B O U G A U T O W Q
F I L B F Y S N P O N B R N R D
A T T A I N D E R L O L O G I L
Q L M F X L A Y O D I I P R M P
Q E H T E L L B C M T S M E V I
E I Q C Y C H F P A A H I S H Z
S T R O P X E O L E T E K S V C
Q F A E B S R U B C I D K O C Z
C U R I C T G A C R P T Y V T S
O X T B A E H B E V A K U J S I
N Q G T R M I V R X C A R D U Y
S L I G D G L P U B L I C I R Z
E O N O B I L I T Y Z S T A T E
N F P H S I C E S S W C G L B I
T A G Y T U D B Y Z N Q O R G D

PUZZLE 07

E C N U G S K J H E D B U R W U F W U Z
F G F A K T A U F R S N G E M O R C H K
B V S I O V V M V R B M P O A V B O R N
B K E E U S I L E M J K B A Z K G N Q L
O P D R V O O C N L O S M A T S T G A E
X E G A O I A N E F T N E D I S E R L S
A B I W D U T W Z G O Z N N G G U E X M
O Y T D Q L H A I I L R C S A T C S F C
H A F F I R M A T I O N R H A T I S T T
M N D M X M D U I N B A E N O G O J P J
F S C E S P T I C F E A A R P O G R E M
B F N M X I I T M Y H S S R U P S M S G
F O U O T E R Z I I C C E W W U F E V Y
M Z W S S O C J R A N S D R E O I D K H
I G N H K R D U N P I I V H P X V U D Z
C O V N P A E N T D C N S R O E E E M F
C C L B E E O P E I U J X H V B R R T K
Y T R I H T K N T P V Q W A E N N K A I
R A Z F T C T E N G B E U X S D B I M X
V V J E X A G K G W B U L B A A U V S Z

PUZZLE 08

130

PUZZLE 09

```
D Z X X J Z L L P O U O P S Y G I V
Y M D D P D R G P A R D O N S F B M
T H S G M M D E N M C M X X S Q K T
T G H R G I L V B B F A O O I Y A Z
O N Z E E T A T S A S X C L P M I B
B I E D X C Z L R S D V J S O W T U
E T X M S T I J L S R E T S I N I M
W N N I H N R F F A I T H F U L L Y
I A M O O C O A F D H E L O S U I F
L R P I I D A I O O T S H E L H M O
E G N C C T L E S R U V I W N D L I
T U Z Y G J C U P S D E H Z D M O B
A N C Y U A G I Q M I I R R G U L A
N T F D L D Q A V R I M N I S Y C F
E S G B F P B T N E Z M A P S F L
S E X E C U T E D X O Y F O R X V T
S B T P S O R N W H I C H H C Y E Y
C B C L E S L U S N O C O R I A B Y
```

PUZZLE 10

```
Z H I N O I T C I D S I R U J Q D
A E N B A L A N C E S P N G I F L
Z M S O I D S W S X R J O Z S O R
D K R Y I A H E H Q W G I D M J S
N G H P R T S E E I D I T E O C S
Z J L A W S A M R B V V U T F O T
D W X S E H I S E I G I T T W I G
T P R N E T D H N P N N I I H H L
X P T T R E A T I E S G T M T N Z
G I I J B V V L K S P H S M R N L
W J U D I C I A L S Q M N O O M P
Q R Q O N O I S S E F N O C F X S
Y G R H R D J Z E R P W C C M N O
L P X Q N Q O R A G T P I E O R A
D B Y Y I G H F E N R S A G C J L
Z Q S T A T E D K O R W D N D A G
I U I U X Q R S K C E H C U Z F U
```

PUZZLE 11

Across:
13. REGULATIONS
17. REPUBLICAN
6. PROPERTY
4. RULES
19. JUNCTION
7. FAITH
10. JUSTICE
2. FELONY
8. CONSENT
1. TERRITORY

Down:
18. IMMUNITIES
3. PRIVILEGE
14. ESCAPING
20. CLAIM
16. RECORDS
12. TREASON

PUZZLE 12

Across:
16. INTENTS
4. PROPOSE
17. APPLICATION
3. VALID
18. CLAUSES
13. STATE
19. SEVERAL
15. RATIFICATION
11. NECESSARY

Down:
12. MANNER
2. SUFFRAGE
14. PURPOSES
5. CONVENTION
4. AMENDMENTS
8. SENATE

131

PUZZLE 13

PUZZLE 14

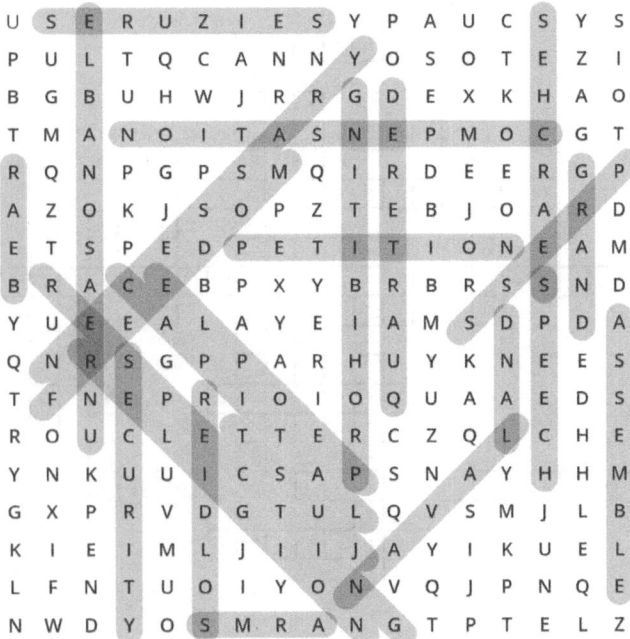

PUZZLE 15

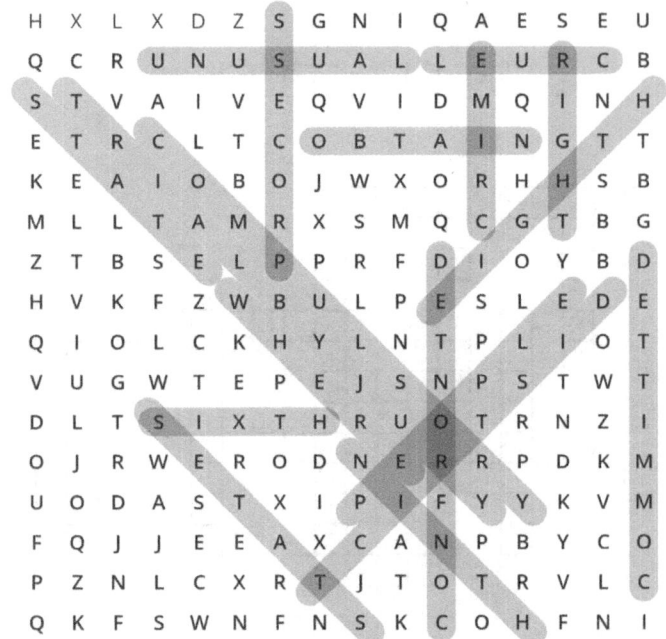

PUZZLE 16

PUZZLE 17

```
Q F O U R T Q A O M K X S O F H B O Y W
V X L E Y T E E F R K B G T L S D U A W
L X B H X E H W Z Q I O C F R T F Q H Q
J V V V R T J K G A H O V O A U Z A Q S
Z T E M P A T L C A D R E W S H O Y S D
T N K J L T W O D U H F T I O Q V C B M
Y N G B P S T O Q S K F A O O V P Z L R
D X C N O C B N C N A F N D V I X G Z U
W S E A R U F S E S I A E Q V N F N X N
I Z G E B P B E I V O G S Z F I P I Z M
S K I U R K T N E D I S E R P E R M M U
Q T N F P H G R H M F Y V N M R E A P R
Y H A I G X T E N J E N E D B I Y L V O
C R R I N V X Z I X D P N L N F Z T H U
E C E K R E P R E S E N T A T I V E S Q
C U H Q L I T W E M R Z E B M B G N I M
I B T B D U A Y M O A E E L D V W Q H T
V T D R A W R H A W L B N R X O X N V J
I M Z L F N S E S L T L Z Z O B K A O O
T F M N H M Z Y Y L K M T K T H I H L I
```

PUZZLE 18

```
S E R V I T U D E C S L J H K L B
L S Y N R N Z P B B D J Z Y V Z P
V M R R Y T S N I X H S W A L E R
T U A O E I X U O N A V O T E W O
A H T B X V L N R I B R W U Y Y T
I Y N D P E A L E R L J T H G I E
P N U E A U C L E V E L T B F A C
R C L Z N P J R S G I C E C F I T
O W O I R J C I O W A G T B T D I
D D V L V F X Z C F N L N I E A O
G K N A A T M G S E N D Z M O R N
L K I R Y U U J E W Z E I K X N N
K C D U B A Q T S G N C S O Q B B
F G H T B L H E V S R U R J V L I
W E L A M G D N H N O D S Y P Q B
R C C N I M G I J J N E X H V L E
L C S E Y P P G Y R Y R O N E O E
```

PUZZLE 19

Crossword answers: ELECTING, INCOMES, SIX, SERVITUDE, FIFTEENTH, THIRTEEN, TWO, STATES, LEGISLATURES, SENATOR, VOTING

PUZZLE 20

Crossword answers: THIRTY, SEX, EXPORT, NINETEEN, SALE, MANUFACTURE, TERRITORIES, INCORPORATIVE, CONGRESS, WOMAN, TRANSPORT, THREE

133

PUZZLE 21

PUZZLE 22

PUZZLE 23

PUZZLE 24

U Z E C R O F N E S X J A R H L A
C Z I H E C S G R C T M P O P Q G
C P K T O G H C Y B A W V W H W I
T P W C S R A E Y W P G O W Q A B
I F N E B T L I U Q N R B C B D A
M N O F L Z L G X Q M U I U M C S
E F T F K C O H F S H T V I C Q W
F X E E O K R T F V I G Y O M B P
D Z L Y R M K E W Z A T U N T Z A
H U E Q D V S E E Q W N O M V E M
R D C O M P E N S A T I O N A N W
F U T Z Z L S N G I Y X Y O R T F
A P I L H A C C E I V Z D G Y C X
C A O A H B D E G D I R B A I C V
M B N W T Y G G I W Y D E I N E D
L D L S E N O C L E A I A J G D Y
A N K Q O R Q O D D R J B Z I S C

PUZZLE 25

PUZZLE 26

Crossword answers:
- LIBERTY
- REPUBLIC
- PLEDGE
- FLAG
- AMERICA
- GOD
- INDIVISIBLE
- JUSTICE
- UNITED
- NATION
- HEART
- FACING
- STANDS
- ALLEGIANCE
- STATES
- ALL

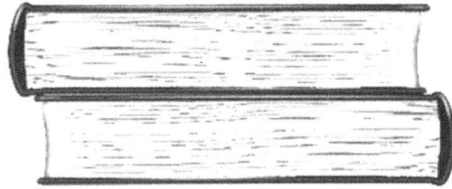

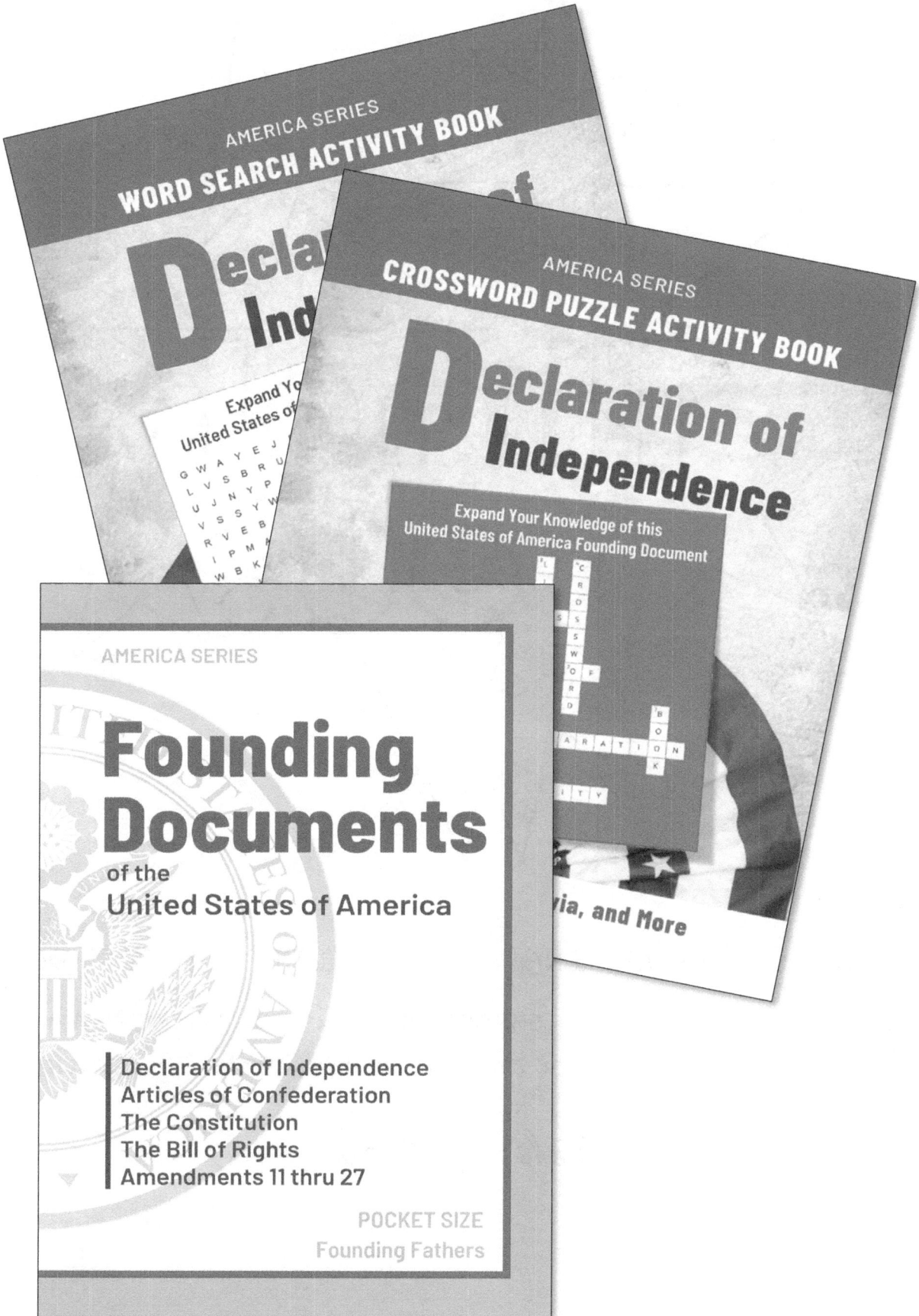

AMERICA SERIES
WORD SEARCH ACTIVITY BOOK

Declaration of Independence

Expand Your Knowledge of this
United States of America Founding Document

AMERICA SERIES
CROSSWORD PUZZLE ACTIVITY BOOK

Declaration of Independence

Expand Your Knowledge of this
United States of America Founding Document

ia, and More

AMERICA SERIES

Founding Documents
of the
United States of America

Declaration of Independence
Articles of Confederation
The Constitution
The Bill of Rights
Amendments 11 thru 27

POCKET SIZE
Founding Fathers

THANK YOU FOR ENJOYING THE ACTIVITIES IN THIS BOOK.

If you have any comments or suggestions that can help us to make our publications better, please email us at **info@AislesOfBooks.club**

Aisles of Books

Made in United States
Cleveland, OH
26 June 2025